Why the World Sucks
and What We Can Do About It

B Regan Asher, Ph.D.

Cover image courtesy of NASA Visible Earth
(http://visibleearth.nasa.gov)

ISBN: 1494277824
ISBN-13:   978-1494277826

Table of Contents

CONSUMER MESSAGE

Some settling of contents may have occurred during shipping. This book is sold by ideas, not by pages.

Information contained herein is believed to be true although, as with all human endeavors, unintentional errors may have been introduced. If you find any issues in this book it would be much appreciated if you would provide the details through the website contact form at http://breganasher.com/contact. Corrections will be implemented in the next release. Please also use the contact form for comments and queries.

Footnotes are provided throughout this book as internet web links. Because the referenced information is beyond the control of the author, it may have changed or been removed since the publication of this book.

B Regan Asher has also created fictional works including "Il Vendetta," "White Cell" and "Why I Had to Kill My Brother."

1. NUTS

The amount of eccentricity in a society has generally been proportional to the amount of genius, mental vigor, and moral courage it contained. That so few now dare to be eccentric marks the chief danger of the time.

−John Stuart Mill 1806-1873
English philosopher

Disclaimer

I love to begin any discussion with a disclaimer. That way everything is on the table from the beginning and we understand one another from the start. So here's my disclaimer: I'm nuts. I'm not nuts like someone sitting in a padded room in a straitjacket or someone sitting in an institutional cafeteria drooling into his porridge. I'm not nuts like the screaming crazies you see in movies or on television. I'm not an ax murderer. Instead I'm nuts in the way you might think an autistic Raymond Babbit was nuts in the movie Rain Main. Even my wife and children sometimes draw an analogy between me and Rain Man. I just don't quite look at things the way most people do. But I don't think I'm obviously nuts at first glance. If you were to meet me casually one day in the street or at work or at a wedding you might initially think me normal. Only after talking with me for some time would you begin to hear some of my ideas ... and then you would realize that I'm not quite like other people you know. Perhaps I'm just eccentric.

I admit openly that I look at things differently. And I understand that my brain is not wired the same way as the majority

1

of the people you probably know. But that's not necessarily a bad thing. It's just the way I am.

Why me?

So that's my disclaimer. With this information in hand why then should you continue reading? After all, if I look at things so differently from everyone else why should I be the one to write a book about the problems with the world? What if the problems I perceive are not problems for everyone else? The answer is simple: because my ideas do strike a chord with others.

When I have spoken to friends, family, colleagues or even strangers about my observations, suggestions and conclusions, my ideas have been generally well received. I admit that on occasion I have been given the polite but dismissive nod that goes along with the uncomfortable smile. And that sometimes I have even seen eyeballs roll back. But I have found that, once I have properly explained my ideas, I have often received the knowing nod rather than the dismissive nod. And I have even seen excitement in those who found that my comments struck a chord.

So this book is partly about putting into words what some people have already been thinking. It's also about offering some novel solutions to ongoing problems. Over the years I've been told many times that I should do something about my ideas. Well, that something is what this book is all about.

What this book is not about

I will refer to some political ideas but this book isn't about politics. This statement may seem odd since politics affects so much of what happens in our world. But as a rule I won't take any one side in a political debate. Instead I will do my best to confine myself to a politically neutral view of the people and the systems that make up Western societies.

Who solves the big problems?

Let's return to my disclaimer. Apart from my desire to disclose my idiosyncratic personality up front, there are a couple of other reasons for providing it. First, disclaimers have become an integral part of my character and, for those who know me, I believe my character provides one of the best reasons to read this book. Second, my disclaimer supports a key principle of this book: integrity. By confessing my biggest personal fault, I'm trying to avoid some sort of subterfuge.

So if integrity is important in this book, what about integrity in our society? It's a great disappointment to me how little our society seems to encourage it; instead we seem to reward deceit, deception and flagrant dishonesty. If you have a car accident your insurance company and your lawyer will both advise you not to volunteer information, even if you know you're at fault. That seems deceitful. Salesmen regularly misrepresent their products to secure a sale. That seems deceptive. Politicians regularly and knowingly lie. That seems dishonest.

We may shrug and say "that's the way it is" but we all know it's wrong. I would make a terrible lawyer, salesman or politician because I believe in bold-faced honesty. It's so easy to say "that's the way it is" but we need move beyond the cliché and instead work to actively promote honesty, integrity and honor. And we need to structure our society to support these principles. Toward this end my disclaimer discloses a significant shortcoming of mine. Better unabashed truth than sexy illusion.

If the act of disclosing this shortcoming supports integrity, then the shortcoming itself, being nuts, is, in a bizarre way, also an asset. Throughout history it has been strange, odd people who have noticed problems and derived solutions to them. The history of science and mathematics is replete with instances where significant improvements in understanding have come from people who think outside of the box. It is also true in nonscientific fields such as art and music. So although being nuts may on the surface be negative, it may also provide a means to address difficult problems.

Admittedly luck also plays a role in discovering and solving problems. Being in the right place at the right time with the right outlook is key. For example, the PBS documentary "Einstein's Big Idea[1]" chronicled several significant scientific advances which came about when special people ignored conventional wisdom. My personal favorite was the realization by Émilie du Châtelet that kinetic energy was proportional to the square of speed. (You may be more familiar with Einstein's later realization that $E=mc^2$.) Don't be smug thinking the result is obvious because it isn't, even if it's now being taught in elementary schools. It had eluded humanity for thousands of years of civilization. And du Châtelet was not wholly responsible for the conclusion since many others had contributed to the effort over time. But du Châtelet made the final connection. She was the right person in the right place at the right time. Perhaps I am too. Or perhaps not.

And what of everyone else?

If eccentric people are responsible for pushing forward human understanding, what of the vast majority of normal people who are good at learning a body of accepted knowledge but not particularly good at making nonintuitive mental leaps? The answer is that we desperately need these people, lots of them, to carry on the business of everyday life. If everyone were weird, nothing would ever get done. Yet we do need a few oddballs, those who can spend a portion or all of their lives thinking on problems that might be unsolvable. For these are the people chiefly responsible for advances in human knowledge.

You're probably a normal person. If so, congratulations. I'm not. Everything bothers me but I particularly hate injustice,

---

[1]   http://www.pbs.org/wgbh/nova/physics/einstein-big-idea.html

dishonesty and hypocrisy. I bristle at even the smallest injustice. And I can get caught up in an angry wrath for days, weeks, months or even years at major injustices. It's from these reactions and many related experiences that the material for this book has been compiled. I simply want to share some of my observations and suggestions. I think the suggestions follow naturally from the evidence but you will ultimately have to be the judge. This is not, after all, science. This is an art. And it has to be appreciated to have any value at all.

Who am I?

Since virtually everything in this book comes from me and not from a committee of world-renowned experts in societal problems, perhaps it's time for one more disclaimer. The name B Regan Asher is a pseudonym. I can only assure you that I am not protecting my own name to avoid something horrible like an arrest warrant. I use it to protect the sources of my examples. Because I use some real life examples in this book, a pseudonym helps keep sources somewhat anonymous.

I believe everything I provide in this book is true, including the Ph.D. that appears after my pseudonym on the title page. I won't disclose the subject area of my degree or the name of the university which granted it, but I will tell you that my doctorate is not in political science and that it was issued by a very well-known and internationally respected university. I'm not sure that makes me respectable but it does provide a little more background on me.

You don't have to agree with everything

You may find that you agree with some ideas presented in this book; you may find that you disagree with others. It doesn't matter. The point of the book is to highlight deficiencies in our society and to make suggestions about how to rectify them. The ideas are just that: ideas. Nothing is 100% and many of my suggestions for improvement are incomplete. Again, it doesn't matter. We just need to start discussing the problems without preconceptions. You would think from all the broohaha in the news that the only problems we have are political disagreements between left-wing and right-wing, liberal and conservative, Republican and Democrat. Yet those are not our biggest problems. The system is our biggest problem and by "system" I include the people in it. I believe people these days are more cynical, less honest and less community minded than even one or two generations ago. In short, I believe people today are less honorable. And that doesn't make for a great society.

But this book is not one of doom and gloom. Quite the contrary, most issues I will raise have solutions. So the real problem is not whether solutions exist but whether we have the wherewithal to implement them. Any problem we ignore today will have to be solved later and waiting will make any solution that much more painful. Best to solve problems today than postpone the inevitable to tomorrow.

I will sometimes give simple examples of the issues that confront us. Don't worry if some issues I present seem trivial; please just take all the issues together to see why I believe our society is on the wrong path. Perhaps by the end of this book you will also feel as I do and want to improve the world in your own unique way. If that's all that comes out of this book then I will have achieved my goal.

You may find that this book is some combination of silly, crazy, preachy and dry. I did my best to balance these aspects. The silliness, craziness and preachiness come partly from my personality; my wife acknowledges the first two and complains wholeheartedly about the third. The dryness comes from some of the subject matter although I've done my best to keep it to a minimum. Drinking water while reading may help.

Finally, thank you for taking the time to read this book. Because you are interested in why I think the world sucks perhaps you are part of a select group that we desperately need: interested people who want to improve the world.

Why the World Sucks

2. HYPOCRITICAL, STUPID, CRAZY THINGS

The planet is fine. The people are [f-cked].

–George Carlin 1937-2008
Stand-up comedian

Hypocritical, stupid, crazy things

There are a myriad of hypocritical, stupid, crazy things about our society that are disconcerting. I'm not talking about hypocritical scientists who dismiss the theory of evolution in favor of an unscientific literal biblical explanation. Or stupid people who apply makeup while driving. Or crazy people who think they're fruit and paint themselves orange. The systemic issues to which I'm referring are hardly debated yet exist in all countries to varying degrees. They could have been fixed long ago but weren't. We all seem to agree they're unfair but we shrug our shoulders when we hear about them, living our lives under a system that we rarely if ever question. But even if we don't question the system, what of our leaders who were elected to improve our society? Unfortunately most of them are no help at all. They are so busy fund-raising, watching polls and horse trading with lobbyists that they have little time to work on improving the system.

So what are these hypocritical, stupid, crazy things? Let me give a few examples now and then relegate everything else to later chapters.

Think about justice. The court system can put an innocent man through the ordeal of a trial, find him innocent, and then ignore the damage it has done to his life. Admittedly this outcome is still better than finding the poor fellow guilty, but what if he and his family become so indebted to lawyers that they are forced into bankruptcy? Or if his career is ruined by the work interruption caused by the trial? Or if his children's lives are damaged when their college accounts are drained to pay the lawyers? We are the system. We did this to the poor fellow. If we don't at least try to compensate a victim of the system, where's the justice? Isn't it hypocritical to have an unjust justice system?

Think about integrity. For whatever reason, we accept that politicians lie. But those whom we elect to lead us need to be above reproach not below contempt. So why do we not hold them accountable for their promises just the same way a consumer goods company is held accountable for false advertising? Is it because without these contemptible politicians the late-night talk shows would run out of material? We are the system. We could have insisted on better rules for those in power. If we don't ensure the integrity of our leaders how can we expect integrity in anyone? Isn't it stupid to select leaders that don't lead?

Think about efficiency. Whether you want big government or small government, waste makes a mockery of the public service. Yet it's clear that government at any level is horribly inefficient. We could have fixed this long ago by simply insisting on competitive fixed-fee-fixed-deliverable contracts, market rates for public service remuneration and merit-based evaluations for public employees. But we didn't. Just look at the recent municipal bankruptcies in the US. It begs the question: why did our leaders not manage an efficient public service all along? The answer is simple: because voters didn't demand it. We are the system. We could have insisted on better accountability. But with leaders who bear no responsibility for mismanagement how can we ever hope for any efficiency? Isn't it crazy to allow politicians to wreak havoc on public finances with no culpability?

Because we don't demand decent behavior of our leaders we

don't encourage decent behavior in anyone. Look at the movies and television shows from the 1950s and then compare them to the movies and television shows of today. Compare "Leave It to Beaver" with "Family Guy." What would an alien landing on Earth make from the differences? That we have degenerated into an unjust, dishonest, inefficient, self-centered, lawless, violent and superficial society? I don't know about you, but I just don't think that's progress in the right direction.

Consider one week in 1997, a week that is a favorite subject of conversation for my wife. During this particular week two well-known international figures died. Diana, Princess of Wales, died on August 31st to all manner of media attention that lasted for years afterward. Not that Diana didn't have her positive traits, but she was more a glamour figure than a saint. Later that same week, on September 5th, Mother Teresa died and, while her death did receive some media attention, the tribute to her was more subdued and shorter lived than that given to Diana. Does it not seem odd that society preferred to recognize Diana over Mother Teresa when it was Teresa who received the 1979 Nobel Peace Prize? And it is Teresa who is now a candidate for Catholic sainthood. Not to put down Diana, but where were our priorities in 1997?

We're not so civilized

Let's leave behind society and the system for a minute. How have we progressed in basic personal behavior? As you drive about town have you taken careful notice of how other people drive? How many don't know the rules of the road? How many know the rules but ignore them? How many are just rude, ignorant people? How many should be put away for texting while driving at 70 mph on the highway? Have drivers always been so inconsiderate or have they become worse over the last generation?

Some of us are more annoyed by this type of ignorant behavior than others but it does seem that our society has deteriorated in several key areas: honesty, citizenship, and courtesy. Since these basic behaviors underlie the successful operation of any society, we should all be concerned about the widespread lack of them. Most people would probably agree that honesty is a necessary trait in a civilized society. Perhaps even citizenship. But to some, courtesy might sound like a luxury. Yet courtesy is actually an indicator of our respect for (or contempt of), not just others, but of our society at large. How much effort does it really take not to cut in line at a cinema? Courtesy is a necessary part of our societal mechanics.

Outsiders also think we behave poorly. Terrorists have criticized our society by describing Western culture as "decadent and corrupt[2]." You may dismiss this depiction as outrageous; after all, why should we listen to terrorists who are criminals that indiscriminately attack the innocent? The answer is that we certainly don't have to accept their viewpoint or their tactics but that not all their observations are necessarily outrageous. Terrorists may depict us as decadent and corrupt as an excuse to justify their reprehensible acts but I believe the portrayal itself is valid. Perhaps our society was not always so but it seems to be now. And we should all be ashamed of what we have become.

Consider how you yourself view society. Do you trust lawyers? Do you trust your local car dealer? Do you believe your dentist when he roughly jostles a tooth until a filling falls out, and then says it needs to be replaced? Do you trust your boss when he says there's no money in the budget for the pay increase he had promised? Do you trust any government official to spend your tax dollars as if they were his own? Do you believe the campaign promises of a politician? Do you trust the automobile mechanic when he says that you need new brakes and shocks when you only came in for an oil change? Do you believe the clothing salesman when he tells you the most expensive suit in the store is the only one for you? Do you believe your neighbor when he says it wasn't his dog that pooped on your lawn? For many of us, our answers to

---

[2]   http://factsanddetails.com/world/cat58/sub386/item2356.html

some or all of these questions are "no."

So we don't trust individuals yet, somehow, we seem so proud of our society. We say we have eliminated slavery. We say we look after the sick and the poor. We say we give each child an equal opportunity. We say that hard work yields its own rewards. We say we are civilized. After all, we can now build taller buildings, bigger cruise ships and swankier hotels. We can now buy diamond rings at Costco. So we say we have evolved. But have we?

This book is not about Utopia; there will always be big problems and bad people. We will always need policemen and jails. This book is simply about ordinary people and about the way our society operates. And this book is about questions. Why can't we trust people anymore? What happened to honor? Would we be better off with the sensibilities of fifty or a hundred years ago?

It's not about politics

In today's politics neither left-wing nor right-wing is looking after the interests of any country as a whole. The right wants to preserve the wealth of the rich. The left wants to steal that wealth for its membership. The right thinks the rich need hardly pay taxes. The left thinks the working class need hardly work to get paid.

It might sound as if this book is political but it isn't. It's not about lowering taxes nor is it about increasing welfare. It's not about right-to-work legislation nor is it about unionization. It's not about conservative ideas nor is it about liberal ideas. And it's certainly not about whether the dinner at a political fund-raiser is worth $1,000 a plate. It's about two basic components of our society: the system and the people. It's about putting civil behavior back into our civilization by correcting some of the injustices that we currently encourage. And it's about correcting the system itself so we can trust it again.

Unfortunately it's always about money

So where do we start? Though it may seem trite to say so, money makes the world go around. So says the musical "Cabaret." Even ABBA sang, "Money, Money, Money." Money is what our system operates on so it seems as good a place as any to start.

When I was growing up and even into my late teens, I was always told that money wasn't the most important thing in life. I was encouraged to enjoy what I did in school and to pick a discipline that I loved. It was good advice, but only up to a point. I did discover on my own that there are many things money can't buy. Money can't buy integrity. Or class. Or a better sense of humor. But I also discovered later that money was more important than I thought, although I'm not talking about an obscene sum of money. I believe putting wealth before everything else is evil, especially since I have witnessed the effect of that attitude on my own family. It's also one of our biggest societal problems. But I did eventually realize that money can buy certain things that society is unwilling to provide for free. For example, money can buy better health … the richest people get the best medical care. In the United States where most medical care is provided privately this should be self-evident. But even in more socialist jurisdictions like Canada or Europe, the wealthiest individuals can always buy the best health care, whether in their own country or abroad. Money can also buy health in an indirect way. Wealthier people eat better, live better and have less stress. Their lifestyle will extend life, if only on a statistical basis.

But I'm not bringing up money just to discuss what it can buy. I'm bringing it up because some of this book is about the way our society gives unfair advantage to certain groups, giving them an edge in earning more income and allowing them to take that income from others. I'm not opposed to a businessman getting rich if he does not benefit from an unfair advantage granted to him by society. He took a great risk in creating his business and no one was forced to purchase from him so he deserves whatever financial success he can achieve. (Note that I'm not aligning myself with right wing politics here ... I've said nothing about the taxation of his income or his assets.)

But those given an unfair advantage, perhaps through a special government concession or a legalized monopoly, must not be allowed to take advantage of their privileged positions. For example, the telephone company has for years had a monopoly that in many countries has been regulated. And rightly so. Without the regulation there would no doubt have been price gouging. If cellular service ever gets to the point where it's a direct competitor to landlines, then regulation may no longer be required since competition would keep pricing in check. But we're not there yet. And there are other monopolies, both conventional and unconventional, which have to be carefully regulated.

With or without the advantage of monopoly, rich people are considered successful in our society. Mean spirited CEOs who receive eight figure bonuses are considered wildly successful even if their success is the result of unethical behavior bordering on thievery. Or sometimes because of thievery. When was the last time you heard of a dedicated nurse who saves lives every day described as successful? A doctor might be described as successful. But a nurse? Not very often.

Everything in the end comes down to money because money can buy a better life, health and power. That's why much of this book is about ensuring a level playing field among the various competing interests in our society.

Animal, vegetable or mineral

I've said before that society is the system and the people. So far we've touched on the system by considering justice, integrity, efficiency and monopoly. We've also touched on the people by considering honesty, citizenship and courtesy. But we haven't yet recognized that there are different types of people. I call these types animals, vegetables and minerals.

We all might well be animals with selfish base instincts but most of us believe we're more than that. After all, none of us wants to be labeled as an animal and selfish behavior is generally considered a negative trait. But few of us are totally selfless and our civilization might not thrive if we were.

Unfortunately we're encouraging animal-like behaviors like selfishness. Wealth, power, fame and status have become all too important icons, especially for our children. Are there not more important characteristics we should value and encourage like honor or charity? I'm talking here about real honor and true charity, not honor or charity with ulterior motives. Even charity can be twisted to serve a selfish goal. For example, why does the tycoon who donates money for a new hospital wing have to name it after himself? Is this charity or advertising?

For those of us raised to believe that being a good person is all important, we were shocked to discover later in life that few others believed it. Or at least few others lived it. How many times have we heard the expression "it's just business" to explain away illegal, immoral or unkind behavior? The murderous Michael Corleone said it in "The Godfather." Anyone who says it is clearly an animal.

So what's a vegetable? Vegetables are people who do not even consider the ramifications of their actions. They are either unintelligent or uneducated, plodding through life with little understanding of or concern for their role in society. They are much like animals, just less conniving. When you present a horrible injustice to a vegetable his reply might well be "so, what do you want me to do about it?"

And then there are those who aspire to be more, perhaps like you or other readers of this book. (If you do aspire to be more this blatant attempt at flattery would have had no effect on you.) These are the gems of our society. Let's call them minerals: thoughtful people, people of conscience. These are people who believe there is a right way and a wrong way to behave. They believe mortgaging their principles for personal advancement diminishes them. They would not embellish their resumés with untruths to secure a job. Religion is no prerequisite for this group. Nor is naïveté. These people simply believe there is more to life than accumulating objects or building prestige, power or fame. They believe that the value of a life is the way it is lived and the way it rises above animal instincts. This group may be small but it's the most important group in our society. And it needs to grow if we are to improve.

I am always pleasantly surprised when I come across one of these gems. It makes me feel good to know they exist. And I know that I can trust them with anything important. Unfortunately they are all too rare.

Good news and bad news

All of us, whether animals, vegetables or minerals, are busy with our lives. Work, family, friends and the innumerable minor errands that make up our day all conspire to make it difficult to contemplate the world we live in. We suspect there is something wrong with the world but we just don't have the time to think about it, let alone to consider how to fix it. Deep down, we all know that the world can be unfair, unjust and unreasonable. Bad things seem to happen to good people and financial success seems to reward bad people. Most of us just carry on as best we can. Ask yourself why Patrick Byrne, CEO of Overstock.com and considered one of the nastiest CEOs in America[3], has been so successful.

So the world is unfair. We've been told by parents, friends and colleagues that, as individuals, we can't fix it. So we persevere in our own lives, ignoring as much as possible the nonsense of the

---

[3]   http://finance.fortune.cnn.com/2011/01/28/nastiest-ceo-lashes-out-at-goldman

world as it swirls around us. How will anything change if we ignore the problem?

The good news is that the world can also surprise us in positive ways. After all, there have been good people in the world. Think of Mother Teresa and Mahatma Gandhi. Or Mr. Rogers. (But not Mr. Robinson of Saturday Night Live.) And in some ways things are not as bad as they used to be. In measurable ways the world is a better place now than it was a hundred years ago. For example, there is less hunger, suffering, and overall poverty.

The bad news is that many nasty societal ingredients present a hundred or a thousand years ago are still present now. Dishonesty, greed and superficial priorities come immediately to mind and we seem to encourage them. We have certainly done little to control for them. Look at Bernard Madoff, not just for what he did but for the insatiable greed of his clients. And because of the improvements to the standard of living over the years, we think we have little incentive to solve the problems that remain. But these problems threaten the very lifestyle that we now think is so secure. This is not a doom and gloom prediction but it is a warning of the direction in which we are heading.

Cut your losses now or read on

Not everyone will agree with every conclusion or proposal in this book. That's only natural; we all look at things differently. I'm not claiming to have a magic solution. I'm not Tony Robbins. But some won't agree with anything. So let me now save time for those who will not be interested in this book at all. If the statement in italics below applies to you then I can save you a lot of time.

Life is too short to worry about the effects our actions have on others. The marketplace should be the sole arbiter of behavior. Take what you can and let others do the same. The cream will rise to the top and the sludge will fall to the bottom.

To those who agree with the statement, good-bye and good riddance. If you're reading the paper version of this book you can burn it in your fireplace; if you have the electronic version you can reclaim some disk space. You can take comfort in the fact that you're are not alone. After all, the Nazis had this outlook, even if it was a perverted version. So does my brother. If it applies to you, go back to your club or office or Klan meeting and find new ways to steal, cheat or connive your way to riches.

But if you have loftier ideals, if you think there is an aspect to our lives that transcends our desires for luxury, power or physical enjoyment, then you should read on. Even "The Economist" has advocated the need to consider the greater welfare of society rather than just individual needs. And The Economist is hardly a left-wing publication. Ambition and success do not preclude good ethical behavior.

Peek ahead

If you're still reading you might appreciate a heads-up, a peek ahead to what's coming in later chapters. I've already touched on some significant and well-known problems with our modern society ... most of this book will be about such problems. But in the next chapter I will deliberately take a detour from problems and criticisms to highlight some of the advances we have made over the years. I think it's important to emphasize again that this book is not all doom and gloom. I'm not predicting a worldwide cataclysm ... I sometimes even need to remind myself that our civilization is not all bad; it's just lost its way.

I will then return to the main focus of this book: problems with society. I will start by setting our sights on a goal, and then drawing comparisons between it and our current system. In subsequent chapters I will address specific issues one by one:

Behavior. We can't trust each other any more because honor has a diminishing role in our society.

Democracy. Some countries are in the midst of a financial disaster while others are heading toward one. Much of the blame for this problem can be placed squarely on the shoulders of democracy. How can the system be rebalanced for fairness?

Leadership. Our leaders and the system can run amok with little oversight. How can we monitor and control power better?

Size. Various levels of government can be responsible for tens or hundreds of millions of citizens meaning that each citizen's vote counts for very little. As a result citizens, with views spanning the political spectrum, end up with governments that can't represent their interests. Can we resize jurisdictions to improve representation?

Politics. Our political leaders, if they are not corrupt, dwell on their individual political ideals, holding up progress instead of working to solve the problems that need solving.

Laws. Laws are so numerous, complex and contradictory that no citizen can possibly understand how to follow them all.

Monopolies. We bestow monopoly powers on groups of people who then abuse that power. And we don't have mechanisms to ensure that their special powers are not abused. Besides the obvious monopolies there are others we don't talk about.

Legal system. Our judicial system is unfair through its lack of respect for and shabby treatment of innocent citizens. How can we be fairer?

Education. Our most precious resource, education, is mismanaged so that some of our best and brightest students are discouraged from contributing to their full potential. That diminishes them but it also diminishes us.

Proposal. You'll have to keep reading to learn what it is.

These problems are known but no one is solving them. Most people shrug and say "that's the way it is." But these problems range from nuisance to severe and may ultimately lead us to catastrophe. We've already seen countries where collapse is a real possibility. This book is about understanding the issues, proposing some solutions and, most importantly, pushing for change. I will also make some suggestions about how to encourage change.

Congratulations

Congratulations if you made it this far, though I haven't really said much that is concrete. If you didn't bail out in a previous section then you must be open-minded enough to consider what is to follow. You may not believe people are entirely selfless but neither do you believe greed should be allowed to expand unchecked. You believe hard work and honesty should be the drivers of society, not a single-minded struggle for riches. You think any job worth doing is worth doing well. You believe in honor and that people should be trustworthy. That does not make you either a capitalist or a socialist; you simply believe in reasonable behavior. You might even be what I previously called a "gem."

So now come the big questions. If the world is so screwed up can it really be changed? If greater people than us have failed, how can any one person succeed? And, more important still, if this book is about changing the world, why should anyone read it if we've been told that change might prove impossible? For the answers you must read on.

Why the World Sucks

3. HAVEN'T WE IMPROVED OVER THE LAST 100 YEARS?

We are at the very beginning of time for the human
race. It is not unreasonable that we grapple with problems.
But there are tens of thousands of years in the future. Our
responsibility is to do what we can, learn what we can,
improve the solutions, and pass them on.

> *–Richard Feynman 1918-1988*
> *Theoretical physicist*

A Quick Glimpse Back

My father used to say, "If you don't have anything nice to say don't say anything at all." It's good advice that I have struggled, and often failed, to follow. And though it's difficult to apply that advice consistently to a book entitled "Why the World Sucks," I will try to do the next best thing. I will dedicate this chapter to a minor review of some improvements we have made to the human condition. I will, off course, eventually list all manner of human deficiencies but those deficiencies will be relegated to later chapters.

Yes, the world has improved over the last 100 years. Medical advances have extended life and improved its quality. Worldwide poverty has been greatly reduced; witness especially countries in South America and Asia, China in particular. Antibiotics, antivirals and birth control are all available to an ever growing percentage of the world population, rich and poor alike. Suffering has been reduced and overall living standards have improved.

But it's not just medicine that has improved the world. Governments have also improved. The Nazi horror of the 20th century has not only been eliminated but the word "Nazi" is now literally a four letter word. South American military dictatorships are all but gone. Communist oppression has almost been eradicated, save for Cuba. And even in undemocratic China the government has had little choice but to concern itself with public opinion, even if reluctantly.

The world is also a more open community with little that can be kept secret though some regimes may try. Television, the internet and affordable travel have made the world smaller than it used to be, reducing the nasty repercussions resulting from xenophobia (North Korea and Iran excepted). Who would have believed even 25 years ago that middle-class Chinese would be able to visit the Sidney Opera House, Big Ben or the Statue of Liberty?

Education, a key ingredient to better living standards, has also improved. In cities like Shanghai and Mumbai where there was little to look forward to just 50 years ago, young engineers are now educated to take up their waiting roles in the new world economy. Worldwide 100 years ago women were highly unlikely to seek a higher education. Today, in many countries, women earn a higher proportion of new university degrees than men.

Sexual discrimination, a historical impediment to female success, has not just been made socially incorrect and illegal. It has truly been reduced in the workplace and even in politics. We have seen women Senators and Parliamentarians, women Presidents and Prime Ministers and women Governors General. It was not that long ago that women could not vote or serve in the military. Such prejudices are indeed disappearing over time.

Other types of discrimination are also on the decline, the elimination of apartheid in South Africa of particular note. In the United States black Americans were discriminated against into the second half of the 20th century but, now, with the election of a black President, a new chapter in American history is being written. Jews worldwide had been treated as second-class citizens for thousands of years culminating in the Nazi atrocities of the 20th century. But the Nazis are gone and minority rights are now protected in many countries.

The elimination of religious fanaticism is one area where the world has not been so successful. Islamic terrorism is probably the best known example but there are also homemade versions of these crazies among other religions and for other causes. In the United States, the Oklahoma City bombers come to mind. But in most of the world such behavior is almost universally considered reprehensible and that is an improvement in itself.

So if the world has improved in all these areas, why does the world suck and why does this book even exist? Because in many important ways the world has not improved and in some ways it may have gotten worse. This statement is not meant to detract from all the marvelous accomplishments we have achieved. It's simply meant to bring attention to all the progress we have yet to make.

Why the World Sucks

4. LESSONS FROM THE FUTURE

There is nothing like a dream to create the future.
Utopia today, flesh and blood tomorrow.

> *– Victor Hugo 1802-1885*
> *French novelist*

The 24th century

One way to improve is to define a lofty goal, and then head toward it with all deliberate speed. Perhaps it's a little eccentric to use the future defined by Star Trek as a goal, but don't be put off by this minor detail; you don't have to be an avid fan of Star Trek to read this book. Trekkies might appear a little odd when they dress up in costume at Star Trek conventions but they have good reason to be excited by the various incarnations of Star Trek. If you are not a Star Trek fan then I ask for your indulgence as I give a quick overview; if you are a Star Trek fan then I ask for your patience.

There are many incarnations of Star Trek: several television series and numerous movies. The original Star Trek series created by Gene Roddenberry was set in the 23rd century and its immediate successor, known as The Next Generation, was set in the 24th. Through Star Trek Roddenberry made several predictions about the future, some minor, some major. Amazingly some of his then outlandish predictions have already come true. For example, one minor prediction was a personal communication device called a "communicator." This prediction was made in the 1960s, decades before the advent of cell phones, so it is therefore truly remarkable that Roddenberry's communicator looks so much like what we eventually called a "flip phone."

Yet Roddenberry and Star Trek made other, more sweeping predictions that have not yet come true. Consider some of these quotations:

> *Poverty was eliminated on Earth, a long time ago. And a lot of other things disappeared with it – hopelessness, despair, cruelty ... – Deanna Troi, Star Trek The Next Generation*

> *The acquisition of wealth is no longer the driving force of our lives. We work to better ourselves and the rest of humanity. – Jean Luc Picard, Star Trek First Contact*

> *... the much maligned common man, and common woman has an enormous hunger for brotherhood. They are ready for the 23rd century now, and they are light-years ahead of their petty governments and their visionless leaders. – Gene Roddenberry, 1976*

Now please don't get the wrong idea about the use of Star Trek here. I'm not making a political statement regarding socialism versus capitalism or left-wing versus right-wing, something I will continue to remind you about. Star Trek doesn't seem to promote any particular political ideology. I'm simply trying to hold out as a possibility a society that made personal growth and human fairness more important than other petty considerations. I would hope both liberals and conservatives would support such a lofty goal. They would certainly disagree about how to achieve it but the goal itself is surely a worthwhile one for any civilized person.

Now let's again consider Star Trek. In Gene Roddenberry's vision the future is not perfect. There are still disagreements, struggles, weapons, and wars. But the general philosophy of the future is personal improvement. Wealth is all but irrelevant because shortages of food and materials have been eliminated. Competition is within: to improve oneself and to challenge oneself to improve the world. While there will always be those who try to exert power over others or to accumulate excess wealth, such behavior is not generally accepted in Roddenberry's 24th century.

Hypocrisy democracy

Why won't our current version of democracy get us to a better future? Because the current system simply doesn't work. And it's hypocritical. Let's consider a few examples.

Some US states have placed a moratorium on the death penalty because of concerns about the lethal injection process[4] and because so many innocent people have been executed[5] in a country rightly proud of its justice system. Conclusion: the judicial system isn't working properly.

Hundreds of billions of dollars have been poured into space exploration projects with abysmal records of success when there has been a shortage of money to feed and educate poor children. In the third quarter of 2012 Lockheed Martin alone spent more than $3.5 million on lobbying, with NASA specifically listed under the section "Specific lobbying issues[6]." Conclusion: our politicians respond to special interests with little concern for what's important.

In most rich countries there are organizations empowered to protect children. These organizations go by names like Child Protective Services or Children's Aid. In some countries these organizations can remove children from parents with no formal hearing or proof of abuse[7] even when these actions violate the key

---

4   http://www.deathpenaltyinfo.org/death-penalty-flux
5   http://www.guardian.co.uk/commentisfree/cifamerica/2012/may/21/america-death-penalty-murders-innocents
6   http://www.lockheedmartin.com/content/dam/lockheed/data/corporate/documents/governance/Lobbying-Report-2012-3Q.pdf
7   http://www.nationalpost.com/news/story.html?id=1690967

principle of "innocent until proven guilty." Conclusion: legal hypocrisy trumps fairness.

In Canada there is a concept of "universal health care." It's a golden rule that politicians are loath to break even when funding shortfalls have caused health care shortages. Simple solutions have been suggested to help reduce the waste inherent in a completely free system, but such fixes have been deemed detrimental to the concept of universal health care. For example, a small user fee for seeing a family physician would have reduced waste without creating a hardship for users, yet such a simple remedy has for years been rejected. This sacrosanct philosophy of universal health care does not even provide everyone with coverage for prescription medication[8]. Or dental care. Even more bizarrely, not all prescriptions paid by the patient are even tax deductible, surely an outrageous policy under a universal health care system. Conclusion: the system is hypocritical.

If our leaders weren't so corrupt and so concerned with lobbyists and the latest polls of their constituents, they could have solved problems like those given above. But because of the way our democracy works, our leaders are not leaders at all. Until that changes, we'll never achieve in reality what Roddenberry achieved through fiction.

Decadence and corruption

It would be helpful if someone with 20/20 hindsight from Roddenberry's 24th century could advise us, someone who could see our society through the stark objectivity of history. But that's not going to happen. So, as a poor substitute, let's consider how our Western society is perceived by outsiders. And what better outsider to give us an unconventional viewpoint than one who is trying to destroy us?

Let's revisit the viewpoint of a terrorist, a viewpoint we

---

[8]   http://healthydebate.ca/2011/07/topic/cost-of-care/pharmacare

considered previously. One of the most serious recent threats to our peaceful existence has been the threat of terrorist attacks, 9/11 being one of the worst. We need not agree with all the terrorists' messages or activities to understand some of what they are saying: that we are "decadent and corrupt." If we take a step back to think objectively about our society, it's hard to argue with this assessment even when the societies from which the terrorists themselves come are no better.

To understand our decadence, think about what our society seems to value. Flaunting of wealth and symbols of status are everywhere. Television commercials tout expensive car brands, fashionable clothing and fancy gadgets that will help make us the envy of our peers. All the while poverty remains a serious issue with malnourished and uneducated children, even in the richest countries. Surely there are more important things than clothing labels for an evolved society to concern itself with.

To understand our corruption, consider that senior civil servants, politicians and multinational executives are routinely investigated for conflicts of interest, fraud and bribery. Should these leaders not be beyond reproach? And if so many of our leaders are corrupt then what does it say about our "system"? We all know that politicians and businessman routinely lie to achieve their goals. But when caught they simply carry on as before, apology optional. And incredibly, even when politicians aren't obviously corrupt, they lie. Just like Toronto Mayor Rob Ford.

Honor

And whatever happened to integrity and honor, key traits of the 24th century? There may be no scientific way to measure the proliferation of decadence and corruption over time, but it certainly seems that our generation is more superficial and materialistic than our parents' and, sadly, it appears our children's generation will be even more so. Surely we should take the time to make integrity a priority for our society. And to instill a sense of honor in everyone, but especially in our leaders and in our children.

The words "duty" and "honor" are used ad nauseam in Star Trek and for good reason: these words provide an underlying philosophy for behavior in the 24th century. They are words with which we need to reacquaint ourselves today. Our legislators certainly don't seem to understand the meaning of these words. Perhaps that's why Americans' confidence in Congress has fallen to the lowest level on record[9]. Yet the military does seem to understand the meaning of these words. Perhaps that's why the US Military is the most trusted institution in the US[10]. How many World War II movies refer to honor? What man or woman would enlist to fight a war and possibly die if not for honor? Yet, in our everyday lives, honor seems to have little place, having been displaced by income, prestige and one-upmanship.

And what of the honor of civilians? In various countries doctors, nurses, paramedics, firemen and policemen have withheld their services as a negotiation tactic for a little more money or some other benefit. While many jurisdictions now outlaw this behavior for essential services, would we not have expected professionals on whom lives depend to behave more honorably and to negotiate their remuneration without holding health or safety to ransom? Would one of the Star Trek officers refuse to save a planet because he was holding out for a longer vacation?

And what about other professionals, like teachers, entrusted with the education of our children? What are teachers teaching our children when they go on strike, not over enough money to survive, but for a fatter pension or another paid holiday? No one is suggesting that teachers or firemen should not be paid well but given their responsibilities should we not expect them to protect their charges over padding their pockets? If money is so important to some of these professionals, perhaps they are in the wrong line

---

[9] http://www.gallup.com/poll/163052/americans-confidence-congress-falls-lowest-record.aspxx

[10] http://www.gallup.com/poll/1597/confidence-institutions.aspx

of work. Perhaps they should simply start a business and take a risk that normally comes with making significant income. Their focus on remuneration is just not honorable behavior given their profession.

My point about the way professionals use extortion for personal benefit is simple: that we've somehow forgotten what's important. Did the nurse choose nursing because of pay or because it was a way to help people? Did the fireman risk his life for a good pension plan or because he wanted to be of service to his community? Did the teacher choose education because of the long summer vacation or for the opportunity to shape the minds of future leaders? Why has money become so important to people who originally chose their occupations for all the right reasons? Did a doctor, nurse or any military officer ever go on strike in Star Trek?

I remind you yet again that this is not a political book. My criticisms of the above professions is not a criticism of collective bargaining since I have not argued here that factory workers or government clerks should not be able to withhold their services. This is a criticism of the behavior of professionals entrusted with our health, our safety and our children. This book is about such behaviors and about searching for a way to manage them.

It's also about looking to the future to imagine the way we would like the world to be. If we set the wheels in motion now, when we reach the 24th century we need not be ashamed of our society. Let's aim to make Gene Roddenberry proud. Or even envious.

Why the World Sucks

5. HONOR AND ILLUSION

Rather fail with honor than succeed by fraud.

—Sophocles 497BC-406BC
Ancient Greek playwright

Society or Family?

In Star Trek, most humans are pretty damned honorable and Klingons have a highly developed, if extreme, view of honor. Honor in Star Trek means working toward the betterment of the larger group, whether it be society or family. Greed is no longer considered acceptable and a job well done is considered a noble endeavor in and of itself. It's truly a wonderful environment. But it's fiction.

Today honor is fading. My parents' generation was more principled than mine while my children's generation is completely self absorbed. This deterioration is evident on both the left and right ends of the political spectrum. Ardent capitalists continue to argue against a fairer tax system even as a higher and higher percentage of wealth concentrates in the hands of fewer and fewer people. All the while the socialists of the Western world continue to cling to the concept that merit is a dirty word by emphasizing seniority as the route to higher wages rather than encouraging personal achievement. I continue to be amazed that opposite political camps can both be so selfish. Is there a political ideology we can trust when no one appears to be considering what's best for society as a whole?

And if no one is considering society then what about family?

Unfortunately even the age old bonds of family are withering and that's a shame: strong family ties and family duty might have gone a long way to solving many of the social issues we have. For virtually every race, religion and country, divorce rates are up and the nuclear family is fading. It's disappointing. Reliable family connections would have given us emotional and financial peace of mind, an enviable insurance against unfortunate events. Even where family connections do exist, family honor seems to now be mostly elusive or illusory, something I have sadly discovered from personal experience. This is not to say that there aren't still some good and honorable families. But they are a dwindling group.

The illusion of brother and sister

When honor was broadly cherished, it made trusting people easier. Today the sentiment "trust is earned" seems more apropos. You used to be able to trust a doctor, a dentist, a lawyer without requiring a character reference. You used to be able to trust your family without a second thought. I certainly thought I could. But then both my siblings chose to put selfish considerations before family and before honorable behavior. My brother put money and control first. My sister put appearances first. Without the details of these instances, you may think them relatively minor; after all, neither my brother nor my sister tried to murder me (to my knowledge). But such simple examples are exactly the point of this chapter: trustworthy people do not pick and choose when they will behave properly; they always try do the right thing. With these simple words we have an acid test for trustworthiness: if you discover that someone can't be trusted, even on a minor issue, that person should probably never be trusted again. It's unfortunate but it's often true. I didn't learn this simple truth until later in life so I lived for a long time with the illusion that my siblings were trustworthy. But illusions are just that – illusions – and I would have preferred to know the truth earlier.

My disappointment in my family has therefore reshaped many

of my views in the last few years. I even wrote a short story about my family issues entitled "Why I Had to Kill My Brother." Though fictional, it encapsulates my recent family difficulties and highlights how family trust and honor have deteriorated, at least from my perspective.

Your personal experience might differ from mine – your siblings might well be trustworthy to the core. If so, great. Because upbringing is probably the single biggest influence on character, it really should be easier to trust like-minded family members than strangers. And historically that has been true. You might also think religion would be a good predictor of trustworthiness but that has not been my experience. My sister was religious; my brother was not religious at all. With the superficial priorities of our society constantly bombarding us, honorable behavior does not seem to come naturally to the religious or to the agnostic, to friends or to family. Rather, honorable behavior is a personal choice requiring a conscious commitment.

Nazi Germany

Consider an example. You are a Jewish doctor living in Germany in 1933. You are well respected as one of the finest medical professionals in the country. You count politicians, lawyers, judges and clergy among your friends. They invite you to their soirées and you in turn invite them to yours. Everyone and everything is very civilized in your world.

Your children attend the best private schools with the children of the other privileged members of German society whom you know so well. You are so well respected that you even count your friends, friends of friends, their relatives and their children among your patients. You have a beautiful home, a beautiful family. A beautiful life.

When one of your friends has financial difficulties or when a charity has a shortfall, you are always there to help because you want to be of service to your friends, your community, your country. You do pro bono work at the hospital for the indigent. You and your whole family are active in a variety of charities.

But then everything changed. And all within just a few years after the Nazis come to power. First you were labeled. Then you lost your directorships at charities and foundations. Then you lost your job. Then you lost your house. And all the while you had to wear a yellow star on your jacket.

It all happened so fast. When the problems first started you sought out your good, close, and well-connected friends for help, many of whom you had yourself helped in the past. First you just asked for some financial help. They were apologetic and they were embarrassed but they were unable to help. They felt it was too dangerous. Where were the honorable people you had spent your life with? Where had their sense of duty to their friend gone? When you discovered that your whole family was to be removed from the city you again sought help from your so-called friends but, again, though apologetic, they found themselves unable to help.

When you finally found yourself at Auschwitz performing slave labor and waiting for an inevitable death you thought back to your friends and realized that their friendship was only a friendship of convenience. It had all been an illusion. The friendships you had were never truly tested. If the Nazis had not come to power, you may have lived your whole life without knowing what your so-called friends truly were. You would have had a good life but it would have been an illusion.

Trust, honor and society

Let's now flip back to the present. Are your friends honorable? Can you really trust them? Have they ever been put to a real test? How do you think your friends would behave if a party like the

Nazis came to power here? Would your friends always do the right thing no matter the circumstances? Perhaps. Perhaps not. One lesson to take from the Nazi years is that trust is something that has to be well tested. Just because your friends are casually friendly and helpful doesn't mean that they can truly be trusted. Only difficult tests prove the true mettle of a person.

That there is such a trust issue is indicative of a society where honor is low on the list of priorities. And it's partly our own fault. We do not properly teach our children about duty or citizenship. As a result we have a whole upcoming generation with a sense of entitlement, a generation that believes in taking what it needs and contributing nothing in return. If honor is rare in our generation, it's a foreign concept to our children's generation.

Another contributing factor is that we do not castigate those who behave dishonorably. We simply chuckle at the dishonesty of politicians. We tell jokes about the sliminess of lawyers. And we really don't try to encourage honorable behavior. Has any politician truly suffered because of a broken campaign promise? (Trekkies would probably appreciate a blurb on the Klingon point of view here.)

As for the general public, how many of us have heard of a baby being dropped at a hospital, its parent unable or unwilling to care for it? Or an elderly parent being similarly dropped? In some circumstances perhaps it was the right choice. In others perhaps the person doing the dropping did not understand or care about honor. That person was simply looking to rid himself of what he saw as a chore. Honor does not come easily but it's this lack of honor that is destroying our society. It's this lack of honor that makes us animals rather than something more, something better.

This issue of honor has bothered me enough over the years that I wrote a novel called "White Cell" about the dilemma faced by an ethical hacker who inadvertently wound up working for the Mafia. He had to struggle to choose between an easy immoral choice or a difficult honorable one. It's like so many choices we face throughout our lives.

Honor is frame of mind which applies to all events, major and minor. The earlier example of the doctor in Nazi Germany is a dramatic illustration that we can probably all agree on. But there are lesser instances that allow us to peek into a person's soul. Do we honor our promises? Do we consider the effect of our actions on others? An honorable person is always honorable, not just when it's convenient. Let's consider some day-to-day examples.

The date

To go by the movies, the stereotypical behavior of a single male is one of deceit when it comes to the opposite sex. According to modern folklore, a boy will tell a girl anything she wants to hear whether or not it's true. This is not to say that all boys are alike but it is to say that it is not uncommon for boys to lie to girls. And, of course, it's not just boys who lie in sexual relationships but boys or girls who lie fall into the animal category. It's a wholly dishonorable behavior that, as a society, we should be ashamed of. Not everyone supports such behavior, but those who do degrade our society. Imagine if everyone simply put honor first. Sex wouldn't disappear. So what's the real downside?

The painter

You need someone to paint the wood trim on your house. Your neighbor recommends Phil's Phantastic Painting, saying that his work is top notch and that he's fairly priced for the job. You call Phil and he comes to your house to prepare an estimate: for $2000 he will paint the entire exterior of your house. You book him to paint your house the following week. But several days later a different painter knocks on your door and offers to do the same work for $1500. What do you do? Do you cancel Phil in favor of the new painter even though you already had a verbal agreement? Or would you honor your original agreement?

Some people would go back to Phil to renegotiate the deal using the lower quotation as the baseline for new pricing. Phil would be given two choices: match the lower quote or cancel the job. Since there's no signed contract, there's really no issue of legal action. But this is not about the law – it's about right and wrong. And giving Phil an ultimatum is wrong, pure and simple. It's not honorable behavior.

If that's hard to see, consider this. Your verbal agreement with Phil was a contract, a personal promise. Phil invested time in providing a free quotation and had reserved time for your project on the basis of your booking. He agreed not to accept any other work for the following week. You, in turn, gained the benefit of Phil's commitment. You had each promised to honor your side of the agreement. To wiggle out of the agreement is just plain wrong.

If you are honorable, is there anything you can do now that you have the second quotation? Absolutely. You can call Phil to explain the situation. You can be clear that you will honor your agreement no matter Phil's response but you would like to know if he can do any better on the pricing. If Phil is smart, he will come down a little in price and remind you that he was the recommended painter. That way you will be much more likely to use his services again and you may recommend him to others. Phil will also trust you because your trust had been earned.

The dentist

For most people, judging the quality of a paint job is easier than judging the quality or necessity of a medical procedure. In fact, how can you trust any medical professional; for example, a dentist? Many of us have heard stories about how, when someone goes into the dentist for a checkup, the dentist checks the teeth so roughly that a filling is forced loose. The dentist then informs the patient that the filling must be replaced. I'm not talking about the normal testing of a filling; I'm talking about a deliberate attempt to generate business. Or perhaps you have heard of dentists who recommend an unnecessary procedure or unnecessary dental appliance. Some trusting souls allow this to go on because they are naïve. Others run from that dentist as fast as they can. The underlying issue here is whether the very well paid dentist has his patients' best interests at heart or only the interests of his own pocketbook. Trust must be earned and if it hasn't been earned we must be wary.

Imagine that someone has been going to the same dentist for ten years before a similar incident occurs. Over that period each time a dental issue arose the dentist looked out for the patient's best interests and provided a number of alternatives. Sometimes the dentist himself would recommend that the patient seek a second opinion if an expensive procedure was proposed. On one occasion the dentist even provided his home telephone number when the patient had a toothache. The patient grew to understand that the dentist truly was looking after his best interests. He trusted his dentist and was not worried about the latest issue with the filling. Because the dentist had always behaved honorably, trust had been earned.

Sometimes a breach of trust comes around full circle. Imagine now that a patient realized he was being defrauded by his dentist. The patient also happened to be the principal of a very good private school in high demand. The dentist and his wife had been desperately trying to get their son into this school but couldn't. Why? The principal had blackballed the son's application because of his knowledge of the dentist's character. Whether blackballing the dentist's son was right or wrong is not the issue; the point here is that honor or lack of honor can also have unintended consequences even for those who don't care about it.

And a word of warning to those who think honor is for saps since I have met many who believe the end truly does justify the means. Dishonorable people are sometimes repaid many times over. The firing of an employee without cause or the defrauding of a customer or the cheating of a partner can be traumatic for the victim. Violent retribution is not unheard of should the pressure on the victim prove too much. Assholes beware: anyone can "go postal."

Honor, a late bloomer

Honor also seems to become more important to some people toward the end of life. Many of us have seen the change of heart in a dishonorable person as he ages. Regret or disappointment in a meaningless or nasty life sometimes happens belatedly. Sometimes amends are made but often too late. During their lives the dishonorable took from others as much as possible, not understanding until too late that it's not what we take from the world that matters; it's what we leave behind. No one remembers fondly those who had the good life at the expense of others; think of Bernard Madoff or Imelda Marcos. But we all have good memories of good people, rich and poor. Think of our earlier examples of Mother Teresa or Mahatma Gandhi. Or perhaps your kindly old grandfather.

Think also of soldiers who fought in World War II and lost their lives trying to protect the best of our society. Would they not be rolling over in their graves if they knew about those businessmen, lawyers, dentists and politicians who have twisted our society into something to feed a personal desire for wealth or power? Is it not shameful that we have allowed this to happen and a slap in the face to those fallen soldiers?

You might be wondering about the cure for this lack of honorable behavior. Better education would help, of our children in particular. It may take a generation to take effect but somehow we have to get our outlook back to what it was when our society was honorable. I will have another, more concrete, suggestion for dentists later.

So why does the world suck? Because we have not only

forgotten to teach our children about honorable behavior but we have allowed an ever growing portion of our society to be dishonorable without ramifications.

6. WHEN EQUAL ISN'T FAIR

A democracy is nothing more than mob rule, where fifty-one percent of the people may take away the rights of the other forty-nine.

– Thomas Jefferson 1743-1826
Founding Father of the United States

Misaligned interests

As you may have already surmised, I like Star Trek for many reasons. Yes, the show can be silly and some episodes can be bad but it can also be very entertaining. Characters might be a little stiff but they provide the continuity of a soap opera. But most importantly, the ethics of Star Trek are inspiring. You may not like science fiction and you may not like Star Trek but Gene Roddenberry's vision of the future is compelling.

Unfortunately we do not live in the 24th century and, even if we did, Star Trek gives little guidance on the societal mechanics of the future. So we're on our own to devise institutions that deal with the democratic failings of the 21st century.

Let's start by considering a fundamental principle of our electoral system. We have all been taught in school that the fairness of our system derives from each citizen having an equal vote. Equality sounds nice and it might even be fair if voters were independent of government largesse. But in most democracies today that is true no longer. Don't mistake this as either a criticism or an endorsement of big government. I'm just interested in improving the system, not pushing any particular political ideology.

Let's consider a thought experiment. What would happen if a special group of citizens votes for a government that promises to enrich only that group? Forget whether this is fair or reasonable; let's just concentrate on whether it's sustainable. Perhaps redheads want a monthly stipend. Or perhaps members of the "Water Buffalo Lodge" want a government-paid pension. Whatever it is, if the group is large enough it will probably get the government it voted for. And once that government is in power the group will not only enjoy its electoral dividend, it will also begin to expand in size as others also seek to share in that dividend. The group will get larger each year, taking more and more resources from the remaining members of society. When cost of the dividend becomes so large that taxes can no longer support it, the government, fearful of losing the votes of so large a group, will turn to debt to fund the ever increasing cost. Eventually the country will collapse under a mountain of debt and everyone will suffer, special group and non-group citizens alike.

Not plausible? Think again. This is happening now in several democratic countries, the most notable recent example being Greece. The special group in these cases includes many of those dependent on the government coffers: welfare recipients, government pensioners and government employees. So what conclusion do we draw here? That when there's a single group which controls a significant percentage of the votes and whose interests are not aligned with those of the country as a whole, the voting system fails us.

The corporate example

Let's consider when something similar happens at a corporation. The Board of Directors of BBBig Corporation wants the CEO's interests to be aligned with the company's interests as much as possible. Historically there have been problems doing this. At one time a CEO was paid a bonus on the basis of sales growth, but the side effect of this policy was a CEO who would chase sales even when the company would lose money. Clearly not good for the company. Subsequently, CEOs were paid bonuses in stock options, the idea being to give CEOs an interest in each company's success: a CEO would only make money on his options if the company did well. Unfortunately, short-term gains in stock price then became the most important consideration for the CEO and he would chase short-term profits at the expense of long-term profitability. Today many CEOs are still given stock options but, to balance a CEO's short-term and long-term outlook, options are restricted so that they can't be exercised in the short term. All these changes to CEO compensation occurred because companies understood it was crucial for the interests of the CEO be aligned with those of the company. That way his decisions would benefit both himself and his shareholders. Is it any less crucial that the interests of national leaders be aligned with the electorate as a whole? No less crucial perhaps, but voters don't seem to behave like shareholders.

The Johnny Syndrome

Consider an anecdotal example. You have an only son called Johnny. He's a bright-eyed eight year old and a good boy but, as an only child, he's spoiled. You're concerned that he should learn responsibility so you try to balance spoiling with responsibility. To this end you arrange a credit account for him at the local candy store but you insist that he pay for his candy at the end of each year from his weekly allowance. The only way he'll be able to pay his annual candy bill will be to exercise discipline throughout the year by carefully saving some money each week. Through this arrangement you allow Johnny to treat himself to candy while he also learns that he's responsible for the costs. You patiently explain all this to Johnny several times and very slowly. Being a good boy, Johnny nods his understanding. Johnny is eight years old ... what do you think will happen?

Of course Johnny will not have saved nearly enough money by the end of the year to cover the candy bill. He may not even have saved any at all. So, at the end of the year, when forced to lose his allowance until the bill is repaid, Johnny will have a good old-fashioned hysterical tantrum.

Why the story about Johnny and why do I call his situation the Johnny Syndrome? Because voters are much the same. The average voter is of average intelligence, average education and average means. The voter will support a government that provides him with what he judges to be the best deal for himself. Or, possibly, the best overall deal for his family. But, like Johnny, he won't necessarily consider how the various benefits he wants will be paid for. He may trust the government to be smarter than he is or he may not care. But he knows what he wants … he wants more from the government and he wants to give less. It's a common outlook. The average voter is not an economist or an accountant. He may even have a problem balancing his own checkbook so how can he be expected to balance the nation's? He's just an average person trying to improve his life.

Euro woes

Of the many possible real life examples I can give of the Johnny Syndrome, a good recent example is the Greek financial crisis. The crisis in Greece, which began in earnest around 2010, is a story of selfish and childish voters, dishonest and incompetent governments and simple bad luck. Don't feel too smug if you think your country is better than Greece. This crisis could have happened in any Western democracy and may yet happen in all of them.

We've all heard about the rioting that occurred in Greece in the period 2010-2012: planned government austerity measures required by the International Monetary Fund (IMF) and the European Central Bank (ECB) had ignited social unrest. The measures, to dramatically cut costs before Greece could access bailout moneys, were required to ensure that the country would be able to service the new debt. The rioting was accompanied by various slogans, my favorite being the one that demonstrates how voters truly do not take responsibility for their choices:

> *I vote, You vote, He votes, She votes, We vote, You vote, They steal*[11].

It's hard not to draw an analogy with the Johnny Syndrome. Like Johnny, Greek voters were simply having a tantrum after being told to pay for their candy. So what happened to Greece, a country that had the second highest growth in the world during the "Greek economic miracle[12]" (1950 to 1973) and growth above the Eurozone average from the early 1990s until just a few years ago? I've already said that the crisis was the result of selfish and childish voters, dishonest and incompetent governments and pure bad luck so let's examine each of these causes one by one.

First, why were the Greek voters at fault? Because they supported governments that gave them the benefits they wanted without any consideration for the eventual consequences. They wanted good government jobs, early retirement and great pensions. If years earlier the voters had understood the ramifications of overspending, the crisis may have been averted. If the voters had understood the ramifications even just five years earlier, that would have given the government time to cut costs more gradually. But since the voters themselves were the biggest cost, they simply refused to acknowledge the problem. The voters, like an eight year old child, would not support austerity because they didn't want to give up their benefits. Nor did they understand that the candy store would not be available forever because the credit line would be cut off.

That brings us to the government's share in the blame. Until

---

[11] http://en.wikipedia.org/wiki/2010%E2%80%9312_Greek_protests
[12] http://en.wikipedia.org/wiki/Greek_economic_miracle

the crisis the government simply executed the will of the voters. No Greek politician wanted to earn the wrath of the voters by forcing them to address the inevitable: that the candy period was about to come to an end. So the government continued to run a bloated, inefficient civil service that employed all too many Greeks with early retirement and great pensions. Like governments in many countries, the Greek government did not bring in enough taxes to pay for these huge expenses and so continued to borrow money to cover ongoing annual deficits. Eventually the financial markets began to lose confidence in Greece's ability to repay its debts and began charging higher and higher interest rates for new money. The Greek government, stuck between upsetting its voters or its creditors, was in danger of defaulting. It had simply run out of money and ways to borrow.

The crisis would have occurred regardless of any other factors but there was also bad luck involved. Only a decade before the crisis, Greece had replaced the Drachma with the Euro so it could not do what countries with their own currency might do. If Greece had been able to borrow money in its own currency, it could simply have printed Drachmas to meet its debt obligations as many countries have done in the past. While this solution may have stoked inflation, it would have kept Greece solvent. It would have also helped Greek exporters since the Drachma would have fallen relative to other currencies. Yes, the switch to the Euro was a conscious decision but it was bad luck that the switch occurred just before the crisis.

Not just Greece

Greece may be a good example of the Johnny Syndrome with voters pushing for unsustainable benefits but the lesson applies to virtually every Western democratic country. In Europe alone Portugal, Spain, and Italy have all had similar, if milder, problems to Greece. France may be overlooked as a problem but that's only because its crisis is probably a little further off. The United States may not be in danger of default yet but its spending has grossly outstripped its revenues for years.   Moreover, in all Western countries an aging population will exacerbate the budget problems over the next generation.   And yet voters are not pushing for more sensible governments.   And governments are not truly planning for the eventual problems.   We will see many more tantrums in many countries in the years to come.

The root cause

So all democracies are facing the same budget problems.   But what's the root cause?   I believe the cause lies in our very concept of democracy.   The concept of "one person one vote" has long been ingrained in our psyches.   It's a laudable concept.   It seems fair.   But in reality it isn't.   Those dependent on the government for their income (e.g. welfare recipients, government pensioners, government employees) can in effect vote on their wages while giving the bill to the other voters.   And through gross overspending, the country as a whole digs a financial hole.   Would a bank give someone an unlimited line of credit simply on the understanding that it all had to be paid back eventually?   Probably not.   A significant proportion of people would spend so much money during their lifetimes that they would never be able to pay it back.   Perhaps they would default because bankruptcy seemed a small price to pay for a lifetime of financial benefits.   Perhaps they would default because they just didn't think of the consequences.   But they would default.   And it's actually worse with voters.   If a voter receives his income from the government through either pay or welfare, then it's like drawing against unlimited credit line that someone else has to repay.   So why not vote for the government who promises more money?   Voters just can't help but give themselves more income whether or not they understand the eventual but horrible consequences.

Today's democracy is flawed because many voters are not objective.   The basic principle of "one person, one vote" simply does not work. An employee cannot choose his own salary and then stick the bill to his employer. Or to his coworker. It doesn't make any sense. This is a problem that no one has wanted to talk about. Until now.

A solution

So what is to be done to solve this significant cause of runaway government spending? We can talk until we're blue in the face about various political solutions to the problem. Right wing advocates would espouse numerous austerity measures. They would cut entitlements like medicare and welfare and they would lay off government workers. Left-wing advocates would look for new sources of revenue. They would recommend raising fuel taxes and increasing income taxes on the wealthy. Those in the middle would cook up a concoction of these two strategies. But we know from experience over the last 50 years that the budgetary problem will not truly be solved until we hit a financial brick wall. And by then it will be too late for a gentle fix.

So, again, what is to be done? I believe the answer is very simple when you recognize that a significant portion of the blame must go to our current version of democracy. The root cause of our financial distress heralds back to the Johnny Syndrome: the electorate is its own worst enemy. The electorate is a spoiled child that can't make the decisions necessary for its own best welfare. So what to do? Dump democracy? We already know dictatorships are not a great alternative. Few of us would be happy with a Hitler or a Stalin making decisions for us. Oligarchies are not much better. Russia and China both have many dissatisfied citizens. So let's go back to the root problem and then modify, rather than eliminate, democracy.

The root problem is that some voters receive their income from the state. Think back to Greece. The voters rioted because they didn't want their jobs cut, their retirement dates extended or their pensions reduced. They wanted to vote on their own income without being responsible for the inevitable shortfall. Government employees, government pensioners and welfare recipients were all voting to pay themselves more than the country could afford. I can't prove it, but I suspect few employees in the Greek private sector were protesting the austerity cuts. And if they were, they couldn't have been protesting too strongly. After all, these were the people whose hard work and taxes were supporting those who wanted to pay themselves too much. These private sector workers were the only true contributors to the economy.

So what's the solution? I think you might need to make sure you're seated before reading the answer. It's a novel idea that some people will consider tantamount to blasphemy. Don't stop reading after you read it because I will have more to say about it afterward.

Weight each person's vote according to whether the voter is a net contributor to or net receiver from the public coffers.

The Weighting Rule

The reasoning behind a weighted approach to voting is simple but its recipe is not specific: the precise way a vote is weighted is important but it's a detail that might need to be different in each country. For discussion purposes, however, I believe the best way to highlight the merits of the approach is to provide a concrete, if arbitrary, example. Consider dividing the electorate into three simple groups of voters, and then assigning voting weights to each group. Let's call it the Weighting Rule.

Let the first group of voters consist of those wholly supported by the state without contributing anything back. This group would primarily include those on welfare; that is, those who don't earn their income. There are reasons why criminals might be considered separately but, for simplicity, let's also put them into this category. This first group of voters is wholly dependent on the public purse for support. Its members should not therefore have a say on their income since it's the rest of the population that is supporting them. The weighting of their votes should be small so, for simplicity and for this example, let's use a weight of zero; that is, this group doesn't get a vote. If this voting rule had been used in Greece, it would have greatly reduced the government's incentive to pursue its reckless course. Those who pushed hardest to avoid austerity would have held no sway over the politicians.

Let the second group of voters consist of those who receive income from the state but who work for their income; for example, government employees, politicians, and employees of state-owned companies. The members of this group don't simply take from the public purse; they provide services for their income. Because they do work for their income and pay taxes, they don't fall into the first category. But though they should have a vote, they are not objective when considering public finances because they can in effect vote for their own salaries and benefits to increase. I suggest that the weighting of their votes be one, with the understanding that the third group will receive a weighting greater than one. If this voting system had been used in Greece, it would have reduced the clout of this group and further focused the government's attention on spending what it could afford.

Finally, the last group consists of voters who earn money in the private sector and pay taxes. Its members do not work for the government and do not receive welfare. Excluded from this group are those who work for government-owned companies because they are really government employees. They therefore fall into the second group. This third group provides all the money for the other two groups and cannot directly affect its own income through voting. I propose that the weighting of its votes should be two; i.e. double that of the second group. Consider the following situation.

An example of the Weighting Rule

Let's imagine that ten percent of the voters are on some sort of welfare, half the remaining voters are in the public sector and the other half in the private sector. Under the "one person, one vote" rule the first two groups would control 55 percent of the votes and would therefore be in a position to control their own wages. But under the Weighting Rule they would only control one third of the votes, making it much more difficult to exercise direct control.

The Weighting Rule is simply a more equitable way of assigning voting rights. Though some voters have less say than others, no one is forced into any of these groups; that is, no one is forced to accept welfare or to take a government job. The lower weights are simply a side effect of accepting government money. Those in the private sector, the ones not paid by the government and yet who fund the government through their taxes, rightly have a greater say in how the government operates. Said another way, they have a fair say in how their hard-earned tax money is spent. It's not unequal voting, it's fair voting. And it's one possible way to mitigate the government benefit gluttony we have been witnessing in the Western world.

In fact, it's the "one person, one vote" system that's unfair. Those in the private sector cannot affect their own incomes yet those on welfare and in the public sector can. And the public group can just give their bill to the private group. It's unfair to private taxpayers and it's disastrous for the country as a whole.

Don't start shaking your head

You might at this point be shaking your head because you've grown up with the view that democracy with "one person, one vote" is the best form of government in the world, that anything else is unfair and that this Weighting Rule of mine is unreasonable. I understand this; it's only natural to resist change. But think about various periods in history that we now judge so completely unreasonable. Think of the periods of slavery in the United States or of apartheid in South Africa. Think of when women or Catholics or Jews were not allowed to vote. Not all of the people back then were bad yet they somehow believed what they were doing was reasonable. Over time, over generations, people began to realize that some things were not reasonable yet it was hard to change because attitudes were already ingrained.

Don't let your attitude be ingrained. Think about the Weighting Rule with an open mind. Realize that it's not like discrimination because those receiving their income from the government do so of their own accord. They weren't born as welfare recipients or as government employees even if their parents were in one of these categories. And as long as we ensure education and opportunities for everyone (I will have more to say on this later), those born into welfare families are not destined to remain on welfare. And besides, leaving welfare or the public service will never be as difficult as changing skin color, Michael Jackson being the exception.

If doing away with the principle of "one person, one vote" still sends shivers up your spine, remember that a truly equal vote has never existed. In the first democracy of ancient Greece all citizens could vote yet only free men were citizens; women could not vote nor could slaves. At various points in time since then, many groups have been excluded from the vote including women, Negros, Catholics and Jews. In most federal elections today only citizens can vote even though legal immigrants pay taxes as well. And it's only in recent history that the concept of universal suffrage has even existed.

So the idea of weighting votes based on the degree of government dependency may well be the fairest way yet devised to choose a government. My example of the 0-1-2 Weighting Rule is not necessarily the last word in how to accomplish this but it's a start. I suspect the vast majority of people in the private sector would agree with me. And I'm hopeful many in the public sector would too, even though it would mean a reduction in their democratic clout. If so, then we may be reaching some sort of social maturity; we would be evolving into a society where most members realize that the best solution for everyone is not necessarily the best solution for themselves as individuals. And that, as good citizens, we must sometimes make self-sacrificing decisions on behalf of our children.

It's this concept of social maturity that appeals to me about Star Trek: the idea that people can do the right thing for their children and for society even if it is not optimal for themselves considered in isolation. It's not so far fetched a concept since we already accept this idea in principle. We can each gain wealth by stealing but if society allowed stealing we would not want to be a part of it. And we certainly would not want our children to be a part of it. The same goes for many crimes universally recognized as bad. Weighting votes is just another way to improve our system so society can operate better. It's just that simple. Ensuring that voters cannot pad their own pockets will help align leaders' interests with those of the electorate as a whole.

So why does the world suck? Because those who are dependent on public funds are given the power to increase their own income at the expense of everyone else. And the consequences of this arrangement are often disastrous.

Why the World Sucks

7. CONTROLLING POWER

Truthfulness has never been counted among the political virtues, and lies have always been regarded as justifiable tools in political dealings.

– Hannah Arendt 1906-1975
German-American political theorist

Power promises

In Gene Roddenberry's 24th century, where people work toward the betterment of mankind, there's little need to resolve conflicts of interest. But today, in the 21st century, we are not quite so evolved so we must look for as many ways as possible to minimize such conflicts.

The Weighting Rule is one way to improve democracy but there are others. If most politicians can't be trusted, especially regarding their electoral promises, how is a voter to make an informed decision? Even if politicians meant what they said, a so-called electoral promise is unenforceable. How long must we struggle with this problem before we address it head-on?

If your child lies, you punish him. If your friend lies, you disown him. If your President lies, you vote for him. What a crock.

It's a shame we allow such misrepresentation since there are simple ways to deal with the problem. It's just that the politicians don't want to address an issue that empowers them. The solution begins with something all democracies have: the independent electoral commission which administers and monitors elections to ensure they proceed fairly and according to the law. This same commission might also deal with broken political promises by administering and enforcing a manifesto for each candidate seeking election.

The concept is simple. Candidates, or perhaps political parties, would be legally bound by promises made in a manifesto and registered with the electoral commission, although they would still be able to describe their intentions verbally without repercussions. Should anyone signing the manifesto renege on any part of it, the commission would be empowered to review the case and would be able to issue a judgment against each signatory. The laws governing the manifesto could be written to be as strict as necessary to ensure compliance. For example, for reneging on a promise to reduce taxes a candidate might be fined or even imprisoned. Candidates would therefore have to be very careful to include in the manifesto only promises which they truly meant to follow through on. The voters would then know the difference between a fluffy idea to get a few votes and a true promise worthy of their votes.

Of course there would be details that would have to be addressed with this concept. For example, there would have to be a mechanism to allow the candidate to break the promise if there were good reason. If the candidate promised a big tax rebate but the economy unexpectedly stalled after the election, he might have cause to cancel or postpone his promise. This could either be taken into consideration by the electoral commission or the law might allow for a referendum on the issue. The details might well vary from jurisdiction to jurisdiction; for example, some jurisdictions might prefer that the courts administer a review rather than the commission.

But regardless of the details, would it not be better to cast your vote for a genuine promise rather than trying to determine which candidate was the lessor liar? Would you and your neighbors not trust politicians more? Would it not give you more confidence in the system?

Abuse of trust

So much for lying to get into power. Let's now turn our attention to abuses of power. This issue affects not only politicians, but many other public servants including those close to the judiciary (police, judges, prosecutors) and those close to the legislators (political advisers, political appointees and senior civil servants). In fact anyone who can affect government or judicial spending, benefits, arrest or detention is in a position of public responsibility and power.

We often hear on the news that someone in a position of power has been investigated, arrested or convicted of abusing the public trust. Sometimes the abuses are small, sometimes large. But regardless of the severity of the crime, there is something fundamentally different between a policeman breaking the law and a civilian. Both are wrong, but the policeman has an advantage of power and respect; it's simply easier for him to get away with the crime. And he should know better, being part of the system himself.

The same holds for a senior civil servant. If the purchasing manager at a private company takes a bribe to select one supplier over another, he will reduce the profitability of the company he works for. It's therefore in the interest of company management to catch him. That's because in the private sector every action is eventually distilled down to the profit and loss statement. But in the public sector there is no profit and loss statement. We may try to measure efficiency or measure return on investment but there is simply no public shareholder whose interests are aligned with profitability. The civil servant who takes a bribe is therefore in a much greater position of trust than the private purchasing manager. And, like the policeman, the civil servant who abuses his position should also know better, being part of the system himself.

So what's the solution to this trust problem? Better supervision and enforcement would certainly help, along with much harsher punishments for those in a position of public trust. Perhaps the policeman who assaults someone should serve twice the prison time of a civilian guilty of the same crime. And perhaps he should also lose his job and be banned from public service for life. Perhaps the civil servant who takes a bribe should make double the restitution to the government, serve a mandatory jail sentence and be banned from public service. The details aren't important; it's the principle of harshly punishing the breach. Trust should be an awful thing to break.

Insidious conflicts

Public servants may, as individuals, try to breach the public trust but what of the system itself? Companies have personalities and frailties of their own, so why not governments? The system itself can be tempted by new sources of income, so when an opportunity arises to increase revenues through subterfuge it's sometimes just too hard to resist.

Take tickets as an example. Many jurisdictions have been accused in the past of using speeding and parking tickets as a revenue source. I don't have an issue with using monetary fines to enforce laws but I do have an issue with governments using these fines as a source of income. Proceeds from fines should never go into general government funds; they should be used for something separate, something which the government will not be tempted to gouge for and over which it cannot exercise control. Perhaps speeding ticket proceeds should be used to fund a trust for those injured in automobile accidents or for the families of those killed. Perhaps parking tickets should be used to fund a special trust for parks or community events. But the disposition of those funds should be wholly out of the reach of the government, to be determined by an independent community committee without government ties.

There are many examples where fines for enforcement have been converted into fines for revenue. How many times have we heard about police speeding ticket quotas? Why should the fine for illegally parking in a disabled parking spot be more than most fines for speeding? When my library introduced e-mail reminders to patrons reminding them of due dates, library fines plummeted. I then learned that our library had a budget shortfall as a result because it had become dependent on fines for its operation. So does that mean that the library should now encourage delinquency?

There's another negative side effect to using fines as a supplement to taxation: people lose respect for the law. It becomes difficult to differentiate a fine meant as a disincentive and a fine meant as taxation. Even in my late teens I presumed that speed limits were set artificially low to trap speeders. As a result, I didn't consider that some speed limits may have actually been set for safety. Sounds silly, doesn't it? But it wasn't just me. Most of my friends were of the same opinion. And my parents too.

Near my parents' house was a very steep, very straight hill with no residences or schools nearby. Bicycles and pedestrians were hardly ever to be seen in the area. Because it was such a steep hill, a driver would have to apply his brakes for the entire descent to avoid accelerating too fast. So why was the speed limit set to 30mph when a higher speed limit was clearly safe? And why did the police like to set up a speed trap at the base of the hill at 9am on a Sunday morning when there was virtually no traffic? My only conclusion was that it was a terrific moneymaker for the city. And that wasn't a very good lesson for any driver, let alone a teenage one.

Conflicts of interest need to be avoided everywhere, in business and in government. Otherwise, the temptation to solve the wrong problem is just too tempting. And we all lose respect for the system. It's that lack of respect that we must try to avoid at all costs.

The ideas

Creating a registered manifesto for candidates or parties will give voters a chance to sort the truth from the lies. Having more severe penalties for abuses of power will focus public servants' attention on their jobs and deter personal gain at the expense of society. And ensuring that fines are not used to fund government operations will eliminate a terrible conflict of interest for the system itself.

So why does the world suck? It sucks because our political leaders lie without repercussions. Because public servants in positions of power are not sufficiently discouraged from taking advantage of their position. And because the system turns fines meant as penalties into revenue sources. It sucks because we have lost respect for our leaders, our public service and our laws. And because our society just doesn't seem to have the wherewithal to fix these deficiencies.

8. SIZE DOES MATTER

*The majority is never right. Never, I tell you! That's
one of these lies in society that no free and intelligent man
can help rebelling against. Who are the people that make
up the biggest proportion of the population – the intelligent
ones or the fools?*

– Henrik Ibsen 1828-1906
Norwegian playwright

Worldwide government

Back to Star Trek for a second. Gene Roddenberry didn't
describe the mechanics of democracy in the future but he did hold
out the possibility of a worldwide government called the United
Federation of Planets. Aliens aside, a world government sounds
like a sensible idea, certainly better than the undemocratic and
dysfunctional United Nations we have today. How can we take the
United Nations seriously when each country gets one vote, no
matter its population? How can we take it seriously when
democracies, oligarchies and dictatorships are all represented as
legitimate? And how can we take it seriously when the real power
in the United Nations lies with a Security Council that only
represents five countries on a permanent basis?

So, yes, we should work toward a true worldwide government
that can look after planet-wide interests. But that's not where the
biggest problems are regarding government size. In fact, a world
government is in some ways moving in the wrong direction. The
problem is that our governments represent too many people. When

a population is relatively homogeneous in philosophy that's not necessarily a problem but nowadays, with the dramatic changes to our demographic makeup through immigration, it's getting harder and harder to achieve a political consensus.

Deadlock

Never mind consensus, some democracies have become deadlocked. One example is the recent intransigence of both Republicans and Democrats in the United States. Hung parliaments also occur frequently in proportional representation systems; in 2010 the British Guardian's Seth Freedman highlighted this problem in Israel's parliamentary system[13]. Obviously gridlock does not serve the interests of the electorate. There must be a way to avoid it. But to avoid it we need to know the underlying cause. What's to blame?

It's hard to blame the electorate, a group of people with average intelligence, average capabilities and diverse backgrounds. Some voters are educated; some are not. Some work; some stay at home; some are on welfare. Some are conservative; some are liberal. Some are law-abiding; some are not. There are various ways to elect a government from the first-past-the-post system in Britain to the proportional system of the Netherlands but they share a problem: the electoral system itself is flawed, unable to select governments that make the best possible decisions for society as a whole.

It's equally hard to blame the politicians who are playing the game according to the rules we have given them. We can blame them for being liars. We can blame them for being stupid. But it's hard to blame them for simply trying to appeal to as many voters as possible when it's the fragmentation of voter sentiment that's the problem.

---

[13]   http://www.guardian.co.uk/commentisfree/2010/apr/29/israel-proportional-representation

Choice of government

In democracies today most responsibility for taxation and spending is at the state and federal levels. Because these large jurisdictions often encompass many millions of citizens, governments are often hard-pressed to serve the wishes of a significant majority. So why not make jurisdictions smaller? Small, independent restaurants are usually better than chain restaurants. And more innovative. Why not do the same with governments and then let people to choose freely between them? For this to happen, changes must occur at all levels of government.

Imagine that two countries with different political philosophies had an open border. Consider the United States and Canada and imagine that the border was removed, that people could move freely between the two countries and that they could vote in their new country of residence. What might then happen? Think about two namesake border cities like the Sault Ste. Marie, Michigan and Sault Ste. Marie, Ontario. Canadians living in Ontario who believed Canada's tax rate was too high might consider moving to Michigan. Americans living in Michigan, believing the US's medical and public welfare systems were unfair, might consider moving to Ontario. As the demographic makeup of each city changed, so too would its political makeup. The US city would probably become more conservative and the Canadian one more liberal. The politicians in each city would then be able to tailor their messages to more homogeneous constituencies. If one city became mismanaged, residents could move to the other.

So far we've just been considering the effect at the city level but most government policy happens at the state and federal levels. That's why changes must happen at those levels as well.

Smaller jurisdictions

Imagine that we now move most taxation and spending responsibilities down to the county/city level. Each county would manage its own income taxes, sales taxes, medical facilities, and welfare systems. If the border were still open between the United States and Canada there would be a true open market in government services. Anyone could move to any county with the philosophy he preferred. If free public medical services were a priority for Fred then he could move to a county that provided them. If low taxes were a priority for Alice then she could move to a different suitable county. If a conservative social policy and strict moral code were a priority for Louis then he could seek a suitable county for those attributes.

There are no doubt a zillion problems I haven't considered on the subject of competitive county governments. I'm the first to admit that these ideas haven't been fully flushed out. But surely the concept is one worth considering: let each small jurisdiction specialize in a particular political philosophy and thereby allow competition between jurisdictions. Don't, however, mistake this kind of government market for a capitalist free market in private goods and services. The government market is one for public services only. Each jurisdiction would still have control over its own economic policy.

Many issues would, of course, have to be resolved. For example, what would happen if someone living in a low tax county without free medical care needed an expensive heart bypass? He might then decide to move to a higher tax county with free medical care. Since he had not been contributing the taxes necessary to support his operation in his new home, the new county might impose limitations on him. But each community could deal with such eventualities in its own way. Some communities might have a waiting period before benefits were available. Some might allow the operation but only if the person committed to living in the jurisdiction for a minimum period of time. Each jurisdiction could pick its own poison. Government experiments would be varied and the losers quickly weeded out, just as in any open market. Whether you're a capitalist, a socialist or a centrist, imagine having a real choice of government and being able to live in a jurisdiction with a political ideology more closely aligned to your own.

And what of the higher levels of government that lose their tax base? They would be restricted to managing only those services and issues commensurate with their geographic size. For example, the federal government might continue to be responsible for crimes normally handled by a national police force like the FBI or RCMP. It might also continue to be responsible for national services like the borders, the airports and the train system. And the federal level might even offer services like tax return processing to each county, though such services might also be better provided by the private sector. State governments may not even be necessary if their responsibilities could be reasonably taken over by either the county or federal levels.

Competition for efficiency and fairness

With various jurisdictions competing against one another, several good things can happen. We have already noted that there would be more political choice and that each jurisdiction would be able to create its own identity, reflecting its demographic makeup. But there are more advantages than this.

Jurisdictions would be able to become as efficient as its citizens demanded. Consider the cost of medical care, whether provided privately or publicly. In all Western countries medical costs are spinning out of control while the requirements continue to grow. In large countries like the United States, Germany and Japan it's very difficult to attack expensive policies because vested interests tend to force politicians to keep these policies. But with a smaller jurisdiction where like-minded citizens demand efficiency, changes would be easier. And this may well force other jurisdictions to follow suit.

So in what ways could we address high public medical costs in an efficient jurisdiction? I can throw out several ideas, though they would all have detractors. One way would be to exclude self-inflicted illnesses from public coverage. For example, smokers might not be covered for lung or throat cancer. The morbidly obese might not be covered for heart issues. Heavy drinkers might not be covered for liver damage. Drunk drivers might not be covered for accident-related injuries. Parachutists might not be covered for their accident injuries. The point here is that limiting health insurance to true health issues will allow better care to be provided to those who do not partake in risky behaviors. Life insurance companies adjust for high-risk activities so why shouldn't governments? I'm not saying these are perfect solutions; I'm just saying that with numerous smaller jurisdictions new ideas could be considered.

It's very difficult to build a consensus to support pragmatic efficiencies today because of the fighting among various interest groups. But smaller jurisdictions may be able to make inroads in these areas. Or even find other ways to improve efficiency. Or perhaps even develop new government services. And any successes could be copied by other jurisdictions.

None of these ideas is a true framework for change; it's just another interesting way to manage our currently unmanageable governments. But in my experience anything that can be left to competition is the better for it so long as monopolies are not allowed under any circumstances.

So why does the world suck? Because governments are so large, they can't truly represent the people. And because it's all but impossible to build a true political consensus, something that we could certainly use today but that we will desperately need in the future.

9. POLITICAL INTRANSIGENCE

*Stubborn and ardent clinging to one's opinion is the
best proof of stupidity.*

*—Michel de Montaigne 1533-1592
French writer*

Deadlock revisited

Star Trek presents a future in which much of the waste and
unfairness inherent in our society has been eliminated and in which
we don't see much political wrangling. In fact the 24th century
seems virtually apolitical. Perhaps that's what makes
Roddenberry's future work so smoothly.

That our own political system is adversarial is actually a good
thing; competition is usually a positive force for change. But in
politics opposing views sometimes become deadlocked, not for
good reason but simply because of pigheadedness on both sides.
When deadlock occurs, it's society that loses. I am not suggesting
for an instant that opposing viewpoints are bad, only that society
isn't well served when the winning of the argument becomes more
important than the solving of the problem.

For those who have forgotten, allow me a moment to remind
you yet again that this is not a political book. I'm not interested in
supporting any political viewpoint whether socialist, capitalist or
any other "ist." I'm only interested in examining the societal
problems we face and the ways we can address them through
structural mechanisms.

From this apolitical perspective let's consider modern politics. In most countries today politics comes down to two basic opposing points of view: the market-driven capitalist view and the humanitarian socialist view. The issue is not about which side is right; it's about how to get opposing viewpoints to work together to serve all constituents instead of just gumming up the mechanics of government. Simply put, by severely polarizing our society into left and right ideals, we've ruined it. It's true that there are centrist points of view which try to balance the arguments but, in the end, even the centrists usually pick a left or right stance for each issue. I don't believe the average voter is as extreme as the political parties; the fact that governments typically alternate over just a few elections means that the electorate itself is somewhere in the middle.

The US federal government typifies these issues: lately we have seen intractability when the Senate, House or President are of different political stripes. How does such intractability serve American society? It doesn't – it's simply a testosterone-charged political stalemate. So let's take a step back to consider why neither left nor right is correct and why it's the polarization of ideas in our current political system that is the problem. And let's continue to use the US as an example. Forget which side of the political fence you would normally sit on. Just be rational.

Health care

The first example we consider is a recent one. The health care issue has been inflamed recently in the United States by what has been labeled "Obamacare." Whether you support Obamacare or whether you don't, it seems clear that the US medical system is broken. Let's avoid the rhetoric and consider some unimpeachable statistics.

*Health spending accounted for 17.7% of GDP in the
United States in 2011, unchanged from 2009 and 2010 but
by far the highest share in the OECD, and more than eight
percentage points higher than the OECD average of 9.3%.
–OECD Health Data 2013*[14]

*... while life expectancy in the United States used to be
1 ½ years above the OECD average in 1960, it is now, at
78.7 years in 2011, almost 1 ½ years below the average of
80.1 years. –OECD Health Data 2013*

These statistics are atrocities. Neither Obamacare nor any
Republican alternative will fix either the cost of health care or the
nation's health problems. A health care cost of 17.6% of GDP is
not only unsustainable (especially with an aging population) it's a
national embarrassment considering the number of Americans
without health care coverage before Obamacare and America's
poor life expectancy with respect to other countries. The only
conclusion is that America is wasting a significant percentage of its
resources. How can any society accept such waste? The simple
answer is that those who have to fix it, the politicians, can't see
past their own petty partisan wrestling. Both sides agree on the
problem; they just can't get together to solve it. This is one reason
that our supposedly advanced Western democratic political system
is broken. Everyone is too busy arguing to take a step back to
simply solve the problem. What a bunch of monkeys we are.
There must be a better way.

View from the left

For a left-wing point of view, take a step back 200 years and
imagine you're a wealthy resident of New York City. All around
you there would have been thousands of poor people dying
because of malnutrition and disease. With your 21st century

---

14   http://www.oecd.org/unitedstates/Briefing-Note-USA-2013.pdf

sensibilities would you not have tried to help them somewhat? After all, their predicament was mostly hereditary – not caused by laziness or ill will but simply bad luck: being born into the wrong class. Would you not shake a little of your good fortune on them? A small portion of your wealth, a portion you would never miss, might make a huge difference to many. Is there a philosophical difference between this 19th century example and health care today? If you would have helped someone dying 200 years ago why would you not also help someone dying today?

Now let's return to the present and imagine now that you are walking down the street and that an elderly woman collapses in front of you very close to a major hospital. Would you not help this woman to the hospital if you could? Would you not be outraged if she was refused treatment? What's the difference between this woman and the millions without some form of health insurance in the US?

If most of us would help someone in need of medical care, why is the conservative right so intransigent about some form of universal health coverage?

Labor Law

A second example is an old one: collective versus individual worker rights. For years, left and right have disagreed about the best way to deal with labor law. In the United States it's very easy to see the contrast by looking at the different approaches on the East Coast between the northern and southern states. In the north the right to collective bargaining is typically enshrined in law. Once a minimum number of workers have voted to create a union, all workers must pay dues whether they want to be part of the union. (Further north in Canada the laws are also very much pro-union.) By contrast, many southern states have what is known as "Right to work[15]" legislation. In these states a unionized

---

[15]   http://www.nrtw.org/rtws.htm

workplace cannot force a worker to pay dues. Each worker retains his individual right to decide. The two approaches to labor law represent a huge division between left and right.

View from the right

For a right-wing point of view, consider a manufacturing environment in a northern US state where a factory is unionized. Pay is determined by job category and seniority; in other words, pay has little or nothing to do with merit. Now consider two workers. One is a 35 year old male who has been working at the factory for ten years. He hates his job so much that his main goal each day is to finish his shift in order to get to the local bar with his friends each night. The other is a 22 year old single mother who has been working at the factory for three years. If she had her choice, she would not be part of the union because she wants to be paid based on her personal performance and not according to an arbitrary contractual pay scale. She wants to do the best job she can in order to get promoted and to improve the opportunities for herself and her child. Furthermore, she attends night school while working toward a management diploma despite the toll it takes on her limited time and resources. This woman's productivity is 20% higher than the man's, although his is within an acceptable (if unchallenging) range. When the layoff notices come out, it's the single mother who must lose her job under the seniority rules. The factory performance will therefore be diminished as a result and all the workers will be at greater risk of the factory eventually failing. To even a socialist or unionist who takes a step back to see the overall picture, it must be difficult to stomach this arrangement. To an unbiased outsider it must seem a senseless waste, not only for the factory, but for society as a whole. And yet, throughout the rich world, politicians seem unwilling to address this type of blatant unfairness. Actually, unfairness is not even the right word. Nor is inefficiency the right word. Stupidity is the right word and it costs us all.

Why then is the liberal left so intransigent about collective bargaining and job security based on seniority?

Where's the solution?

Political intransigence is a difficult problem to solve. One possible solution was discussed in the previous chapter: smaller jurisdictions. By creating jurisdictions small enough to specialize in a particular political philosophy, intransigence on the most important topics might no longer be an issue. Different jurisdictions can then make opposite decisions, satisfying their own unique constituencies. There will always be some topics that polarize a constituency but smaller, more focused jurisdictions should minimize deadlock.

So why does the world suck? Because in our world, even when we all agree there's a problem, we can't solve it because of petty bickering.

10. THE RULE OF LAW

If you have ten thousand regulations you destroy all respect for the law.

—Winston Churchill 1874-1965
British Prime Minister

Too many laws

The 24th century portrayed by Star Trek isn't Utopia. There are still laws that must be obeyed, criminals to be judged, prisoners to incarcerate. But that should come as no surprise; humanity ain't perfect. We don't need a glimpse of the future to know that we'll always need the rule of law. We know from history that not everyone is going to follow even the most basic of laws, those fundamental rules which have existed for thousands of years and across a myriad different societies.

The basic laws to which I refer are those that the vast majority of the population would agree are absolutely necessary for the civilized operation of society. Obvious examples are laws against murder and theft, which have been prohibited throughout the ages. Without such laws there would be chaos. And they are straightforward to implement because virtually everyone can agree on them. And, more importantly, can understand them.

We can probably all agree that prohibiting murder and theft are two very good laws to have on the books and that it's worth the cost of the judicial and enforcement infrastructure to deal with them: courts, lawyers, police, etc. But how many laws do we really need? It seems today that we have a law for everything.

Personally, I'm worried that I'm eventually going to need a permit to pee!

Laws are too complex

The sheer number of laws is one problem. But their complexity is another. Some laws can run to thousands of pages as we will see later. In some cases legislators themselves have not read their own laws in their entirety. So what have we done by enacting such laws? Instead of protecting the smooth operation of our society with restrictions we all agree are absolutely necessary, we've created a battalion of government workers and lawyers whose sole function is to write, read, and understand these complex laws. The average person has little or no hope of understanding their intricacies. Even a legal expert has little hope of fully understanding an unwieldy law without dedicating significant time to the effort.

These complex laws make a mockery of a society that prides itself on fairness. When laws are so complex that the average person cannot understand them, how can anyone be expected to be held accountable for breaking them? Ignorance of the law is rightly not considered an excuse but what if the law can't be understood? It's just not right. It's idiotic.

And complexity brings with it many other negative side effects. One side effect is the financial cost to society. To ensure compliance with complex laws, companies and individuals must enlist costly legal advice in order to understand how the laws affect them. Personally, I'd rather pay for a nice dinner out than pay my lawyer and accountant to determine if that dinner is tax deductible.

Another side effect of complexity is how it undermines the rule of law when good, law-abiding people begin to ignore laws or, worse, ridicule them precisely because of their complexity. A good recent example is the health care law enacted by the Obama administration in the US. Whether you are for or against this law doesn't matter. The press had a field day just trying to find legislators who had actually read it in its entirety[16]. Pages of regulations related to the law have been counted as running anywhere from 13,000 to 40,000 pages[17]. It's not healthy for democracy when people begin to poke fun at the system itself. It's a slippery slope toward anarchy. What finally undermines the rule of law is when normally law-abiding citizens lose respect for it. Why should a citizen believe laws should be followed when they seem to hold no personal relevance?

A third side effect of complexity are the errors that are inevitably introduced. Long, complex laws will always be error prone. Just like bugs in a large computer program, it's inevitable that complex laws will not perfectly encapsulate the intent of the legislators. When the errors in the law become known, the benefit of the original intent may be lost.

Finally, complexity affects the legal system by gumming up its operation. Slow justice is no justice and everyone loses.

Yet complexity is only part of the problem. Laws are now enacted for issues which could be much more effectively be managed in other ways.

Laws can be stupid

Consider Ontario's Drive Clean[18] law, enacted to improve air quality in the most populous part of the province. It mandates that older cars pass an emissions test every two years, so if your car pollutes above the legal limit you must fix it before you can renew the license plate.

---

16 http://washingtonexaminer.com/obamacares-2700-pages-are-too-much-for-justices/article/1204606

17 http://www.washingtonpost.com/blogs/fact-checker/post/how-many-pages-of-regulations-for-obamacare/2013/05/14/61eec914-bcf9-11e2-9b09-1638acc3942e_blog.html

18 http://www.ene.gov.on.ca/environment/en/category/drive_clean/STDPROD_1030 62

Yet if your car pollutes so much that the repair cost is estimated at more than $450, then you will receive a Conditional Pass and will be allowed to continue polluting. And you can continue polluting for as long as you own the car as long as you continue to receive a Conditional Pass after each test.

This Conditional Pass doesn't make the law particularly fair, does it? If my car costs $400 to repair I must spend the money. But if yours costs $500 you don't. Doesn't that make a mockery of the stated goal of reducing emissions?

Reserved seating

Let's look back to the 1970s and consider the relatively minor issue of seating for the elderly and disabled on city buses. Back then we were all taught to give up our seats to these passengers. We were taught that it was the considerate thing to do and that it was good citizenship. And back then it seemed to work.

In later years interior signs were posted in the buses requesting that passengers give up their seats for elderly and disabled passengers. It was a shame these signs were required; passengers should have been able to do what previous generations did. But the signs probably didn't do any harm.

Unfortunately the message on the signs was eventually changed in some jurisdictions from a request to a legal requirement. Seats at the front of the bus became reserved for elderly and disabled passengers by law. This was a legal requirement backed up with a fine. That's a shame. We turned a good lesson in citizenship, where each person did the right thing and felt good about doing it, into a law. I myself remember occasions as a child where I gave up my seat for an elderly person and I did feel good about it. It was no big deal but it did make me feel as if I had accomplished something important. Today no one has the opportunity to be considerate since the elderly and disabled have their own seats. Should there be a shortage, would any of our new generation of children want to give up their seats? Worse still, what happens when there are too many reserved seats. On packed buses with standing room only these reserved seats may go empty since they are reserved for people who aren't there. This is hardly an efficient use of resources. My grandparents wouldn't have been impressed.

Reserved parking spaces

A related issue is that of disabled spaces in parking lots. In many jurisdictions there are now laws specifying the number of parking spaces that must be reserved for disabled drivers or passengers. And there is usually a large fine levied for anyone parking in a reserved spot without a permit. For example, in 2013 the fine for parking in a handicapped space in Ontario, Canada was $450. By contrast, the minimum fine for careless driving was $400. It's hard to fathom how a serious charge like driving carelessly can incur a smaller fine that a relatively minor infraction like illegal parking. Disabled parking is just another law that's poorly conceived. The idea of helping the disabled is noble; it's the law that's bad.

The specific number of disabled parking spaces reserved at each parking lot is sometimes specified relative to the total number of parking spaces. But some parking lots, by virtue of their location, see few disabled drivers. Some see many. Consider the parking lot at a hockey equipment store where a relatively small percentage of patrons are disabled. Or consider the parking lot at a geriatric medical center or prosthetic device store where a large percentage of the patrons are disabled. Or consider two retailers, one of which provides a seniors' discount and the other which caters to teenagers. Their clienteles are very different. As a result, there's often a misallocation of disabled parking spaces. What a waste of resources and a senseless cost for the businesses and their customers to bear.

So what if there were no law? After all, the purpose of this book is not to make life more difficult for the disabled; the purpose is to improve fairness and efficiency for everyone. Without the law, each store or office or business could decide how many disabled spaces to reserve for its customer base. In fact, with modern technology like electronic signs it's even possible to vary the number of spaces by day or time to suit traffic patterns. You might object to giving businesses control of their disabled parking spaces, thinking businesses wouldn't rise to the occasion. But there is proof they will. Many retailers now provide reserved parking spaces for pregnant women or families with young children. Some provide parking spaces for hybrid vehicles. These spaces are provided voluntarily as a service to their customers, not because of a legal requirement.

And what about enforcement? If we were a better society, more respectful of others as we were just 50 years ago, enforcement of disabled parking spots wouldn't be required. Even today, I suspect few people would choose to violate the rule. But if enforcement were required, private lot owners do have the power to enforce their own rules by having violators towed away.

What else would legislators do?

If lot owners can specify and enforce their own parking rules for disabled parking, then why did we write the law at all? The problem is legislative diarrhea. Our legislators just seem to thrive on making laws and there are a few reasons why I think they do:

1. When a special interest group pushes for law that on the surface seems noble, few legislators want to say "no" for fear of being labeled unsympathetic.

2. Legislators seem to think enacting any law with a low possibility of negative publicity makes them seem productive.

3. Many legislators seem to favor government control over individual freedom. (This is a little less evident in the US

than in other Western countries since there tends to be a greater American affinity for individual freedom. However, even the US now seems to be moving toward more government control.)

Laws for the disabled are just one example of legislative diarrhea. I chose it because it's an easy one to understand and because there are better non-legislative alternatives; for example, allowing parking lot owners to make their own rules. Again, this example was not about reducing access to disabled parking; it was about looking for the best solution to a problem.

But disabled parking places are not a significant problem for most people. So what's an example of a law that affects almost everyone and is universally accepted as too complex? That's easy: tax law.

Tax laws

To truly understand the problem with tax laws you need to forget everything you know about taxes and take a step back. Consider what would make the most sense if you were to start a personal tax regime from scratch. Leave politics out of it; that is, don't worry about the actual tax rates or whether they're tiered or flat. Don't worry about what the taxes would be used for. On this basis I believe most people would agree with the following minimal guidelines:

1. Less income incurs less tax.

2. The minimum income needed for basic survival is not taxed.

3. The filing of an annual tax return should be so simple an exercise that the majority of taxpayers would not choose to pay for assistance from a 3rd party.

4. No optimization of taxes should be possible; no one should be able to buy himself a lower tax bill by hiring an

accountant or by purchasing software.

5. All tax deductions are automatic; there's no need to opt-in to a program that reduces or rebates tax.

6. A taxpayer with a highly variable income over several years (e.g. artists, commissioned salespeople) should not be penalized relative to someone with steady income.

7. A family should not pay more tax than the total taxes payable for all its members as individuals.

Note that these guidelines are not aligned with a specific political philosophy since they don't, except in the most trivial way, address the details of tax rates or how tax revenues are spent.

So how are our societies doing relative to these guidelines? We need an example so let's use Canada, a country that seems to be fairly centrist politically, somewhere in the middle between the US and Europe.

How do Canada's tax laws conform with the above guidelines? Would it surprise you to learn that Canadian tax laws break every single one of them? You may not agree with all the guidelines but you probably accept the majority of them. How then can a supposedly civilized country like Canada with a reputation for fairness treat its taxpayers so shabbily? Let's first see how Canada breaks the guidelines:

1. *Less income incurs less tax:* Like some other jurisdictions, Canada currently taxes capital gains at a lower rate than other types of income. In Canada capital gains are taxed at half the normal rate. Consider a simplified, if extreme, example. Fred, through luck or design, earns only capital gains income. Bill's taxable income is 25% lower than Fred's but is free of capital gains. Ignoring tax credits, if Bill and Fred both pay the lowest marginal tax rate, Bill will pay 50% more taxes than Fred even though he earned less.

2. *The minimum income needed for basic survival is not taxed:* In 2011 the Low Income Cut-Off (LICO) in Canada[19] for a single person living in a large city was $23,298 before taxes. The equivalent LICO after taxes was $19,307, meaning that the Canadian government allowed almost $4,000 in taxes for someone earning the LICO. It's thus possible in Canada to pay taxes yet not have enough income for basic survival.

3. *The filing of an annual tax return should be so simple an exercise that the majority of taxpayers would not choose to pay for assistance from a 3rd party:* According to the Financial Consumer Agency of Canada, almost 60 percent[20] of Canadians filed electronic income tax returns in 2009 using tax software or a tax adviser. And that percentage doesn't include those who used tax software yet filed their income tax on printed forms.

4. *No optimization of taxes should be possible:* But optimization is possible. Canadian tax advisers and tax software companies tout their ability to optimize the tax bill.

5. *All tax reductions are automatic:* Canada has opt-in programs to lower or refund taxes. One of the best-known is the GST/HST rebate. If you don't know about it or don't remember to opt-in then you don't get it.

6. *Taxpayers with highly variable incomes over more than a fiscal year should not be penalized:* Canada used to have a tax averaging method allowing those with highly variable incomes to smooth out their income over several years for tax purposes but this feature has been gone for a long time. Those with variable incomes like artists are therefore gouged in high income years because of the marginal tax

---

[19] http://www5.statcan.gc.ca/cansim/pick-choisir?lang=eng&p2=33&id=2020801
[20] http://www.fcac-acfc.gc.ca/Eng/resources/educationalPrograms/ft-of/Pages/taxes-qc-4-5.aspx

rate system; they therefore often pay more over a multiyear period than someone with a more constant income profile.

7. *Families should not pay more tax than the total taxes payable for all its members as individuals:* In Canada married couples can pay more taxes than they would as individuals[21]. Furthermore, as individuals they would also be entitled to tax-free gains on one residence each; as a married couple they would only be entitled to a single tax-free residence.

Not a very impressive result for Canada on the basic tax guidelines, is it? Tax law is an example of laws that have become so complex and unfair that few people truly understand them. Because most countries' tax laws have evolved over time, ongoing revisions have exacerbated the problem.

Perhaps it's time to consider how to minimize the number of laws we have and their complexity. Perhaps we should consider a constitutional set of guidelines to ensure that we only legislate that which is absolutely necessary and keep necessary laws as simple as possible. I'm sure this idea creates a whole new set of problems but surely it's time to make sure our laws are truly necessary, fair and as straightforward as possible.

Reduce and simplify

While it's true that reducing the number of laws may hurt our ability to regulate society, surely our goal should be a society that regulates itself as much as possible. Where the need is great and where there is no alternative, certainly let the legislators step in.

If the tax code were ridiculously simple: few or no deductions, few tax tiers and a trivial tax return, imagine the effect on our society. Ordinary people would bear less resentment toward the rich since the rich would no longer use accountants and lawyers to

---

21   http://nawl.ca/en/money/living-with-a-partner-know-your-rights-and-responsibilities

exploit loopholes in the law. Everyone would fill in his own tax return, knowing full well that his tax bill was correct. Personal tax accountants and tax services would not longer be required; numerically literate accountants could do useful work instead of nonsense paper shuffling. They could be much better deployed as business accountants or in a different, more productive field altogether. Their existence exploiting arbitrary tax loopholes would be a thing of the past. And our economy would not have to support an entire industry dedicated to avoiding tax.

This chapter was about our laws and not about social policy. It wasn't about whether disabled people should have special parking spaces or whether our taxes should be higher or lower. It was about devising a system that doesn't waste our time or resources senselessly. And it was about removing inflexible laws that are overkill for what needs to be achieved. Let the merchant regulate disabled spots for his own customers. Let the calculation of taxes be simple and fair for everyone, no matter his resources or capabilities. If the government wants to encourage certain types of spending or saving behaviors, let the incentives be obvious and painless for the average citizen instead of complicating everyone's life with a horrendous tax regime. There is an old acronym that governments would do well to remember, KISS: Keep It Simple Stupid.

So why does the world suck? It sucks because we're wasting resources on unnecessary and overly complex laws. And our citizens are losing respect for the law. Imagine if all the money we spend as a society on wasted parking spaces, tax accountants and a myriad other things was available for parks, recreation, feeding poor children or simply to be put back into our own pockets. I'd use the money to eat out at restaurants more often. Wouldn't that be a better world?

Why the World Sucks

11. MONOPOLIES

I don't know what a monopoly is until somebody tells me.

−Steve Ballmer 1956-
Microsoft CEO

The monopolies you already know and hate

I'm not sure Gene Roddenberry depicted any monopolies but, if he did, they would probably have behaved well. Such is the benefit of fiction.

Monopolies are a funny thing. They are companies or groups or organizations that, because they hold significant control over a product or service, are in a position to stifle competition. They make it very difficult for others to offer competing products. Even dyed-in-the-wool capitalists understand the need to curtail their power. We've all heard about specific monopolies that governments had to regulate. Examples include Standard Oil, Microsoft and Google. These were private companies that had managed, through various means, to achieve a stranglehold on an industry: Standard Oil in energy, Microsoft in operating systems and Google in internet search. For Microsoft and Google, their monopolies were worldwide so more than one country was involved in their regulation.

There are other examples of monopolies that exist, not because they were able control an obscene market share in their industry, but because a government bequeathed them special powers. Telephone and cable companies are good examples of these types of monopolies because they have held regional control over the physical wiring that connects households and businesses. Historically it's been impractical to have more than one competing company provide this "last mile" of service to the customer. In many Western countries, telephone and cable companies have therefore been regulated to ensure reasonable service and pricing for consumers in the absence of competition.

Today telephone and cable companies continue to have monopolies but are a little weaker because of the proliferation of cellular telephone and wireless internet services. This does not eliminate the need for regulation but it does give the consumer more choices. One might ask if regulation could have been avoided if these companies had been more honorable; i.e. should there not be a business-like parallel of the individual honor I have be espousing? But this is unfair. A company's prime motivation is to make money for its shareholders subject to the needs of its customers and the laws of the land. One reason that companies cannot be expected to operate honorably is because they are not all owned by individuals. Management must therefore concern itself with a single goal: to serve the financial interests of its owners. That's why we need rules for businesses to help them balance the needs of their shareholders with the needs of society.

We still might ask the question: why do monopolies not operate in the interests of society if they know they will eventually be regulated? Perhaps the answer is related to a famous quotation from Lord Acton, the English historian, politician and writer:

> *Power tends to corrupt, and absolute power corrupts absolutely. Great men are almost always bad men.*
>
> *– Lord Acton*

Because monopolies have a virtual carte blanche to charge or do whatever they want within their industry, it's virtually impossible for them to self-regulate. They may even begin to believe it is their right to behave as they do. Even now with regulations, some of the worst service in the Western world comes from telephone and cable companies that just can't shake the idea that they rule their roost. Well-known monopolies like these have already been regulated. But they are not the only ones of concern.

The quasopolies

There are also companies that behave like monopolies even though, strictly speaking, they aren't. These companies may not have complete control of an industry but they control such a share that their behavior is virtually unchallenged.

My favorite example of such a company is an American retailer that is a household name and whose exploits are well-known. I have a decent knowledge of this retailer because I dealt with the company when I worked for a supplier to the retail sector. I have also read about the retailer's history and about its founder. I find its history interesting because I believe the company started out as a good example of retail excellence. The founder was dedicated in his belief that his customers deserved the best prices and services he could provide. Though he had always emphasized aggressive negotiations with suppliers, from what I've been able to ascertain he always kept his word. I believe that, until relatively recently, this retailer was indeed a good, honest company and a positive force for the economy.

When the company lost its founder, it changed and it was after this point that I began to deal with the company on behalf of one of its suppliers. In my initial dealings it still seemed relatively well and fairly run. For example, it maintained strict conflict of interest guidelines for its buyers when virtually all its competitors turned a blind eye to bribery. However, over my first five years of dealing with the company, its behavior deteriorated dramatically. Perhaps it had grown too fast or perhaps it had lost its way. I suspect that the senior managers did not have the vision or the ability to grow the company the way the founder had. And, besides, growth had become much more difficult for the company as it became a bigger and bigger player in the marketplace.

In the years following my first dealings with the company it became a consummate manipulator. It created new fad-like strategies made for consumption by a naïve public. The company always promised openness and honesty with its suppliers but in my dealings I found these promises to be nothing but smoke and mirrors. The company would sometimes negotiate verbal rather than written agreements and would then renege on them. Such tactics were very hard on smaller suppliers, some of which eventually went broke. The company's relationship with its employees became infamous, echoing the unethical tactics used with suppliers. As pricing became the sole driving force for the company, quality and safety seemed to receive less consideration. The company was also one of the biggest drivers to offshore manufacturing, a strategy that helped it in the short-term but probably hurt its home country in the long term.

In discussing the retailer with other suppliers I found a complete lack of respect for it or its operating principles. Its hypocrisy and unethical behavior was driving good, ethical suppliers out of business. And yet there was little to be done when the company virtually controlled the low end of the retail spectrum. If a supplier complained, it would risk being shut out from a significant portion of the retail landscape. For some suppliers, the retailer had become the largest customer. The suppliers, no matter how well they performed, were stuck.

Employees fared no better. I recall that I was once asked to help a new store set up a department. When I found the department manager I asked how I could be of assistance but she replied that she didn't know and didn't care. "I hate this job," she said to me. After the store manager came by to introduce himself, she told me that he was an idiot. One anecdote does not prove that the employees were hard done by, yet I heard these types of remarks often when I would check the stock of our products at various stores.

So, was the company a monopoly? No, not in a strict sense. But with a significant portion of the low-end retail market and unfair purchasing and employment policies, this was a company that needed to be regulated. Regulation of this company would not be an attempt to control the private sector; it would be an effort to supervise a too-powerful company that was abusing a sector of the economy. The same would apply to any company that exercised unreasonable control over any economic sector. I call these companies "quasopolies."

If you're interested in understanding more about where I believe quasopolies are heading, I shamelessly suggest reading "Il Vendetta," a novel about the largest retailer in the world. It's fiction but it's my prediction of where companies like the retailer I described above are headed.

The monopolies you didn't know about

Before I discuss an insidious set of monopolies, let's remind ourselves what democracy is all about. The word democracy comes from the Greek word "demokratia," meaning "people power." "The people" control everything: laws, property, rights. No one group supersedes the people as a whole. Yet, as a society, we have given virtually unlimited monopolistic powers to several groups of people. And our governments have made little effort to regulate these groups. So who are they? They are what we call professionals.

"What?" you may ask. "Professionals? Like doctors, lawyers, accountants, dentists and engineers?"

"Yep," I answer. "Never would have guessed, would you?"

There are many professions that behave like monopolies but, for the purposes of illustration, let's choose dentists as an example. Dentists as a group are given a monopoly just like the telephone company. In North America, dental associations control the accreditation of dental education programs where dentists are educated (naturally) by other dentists. Licensing Boards (which go by various names; for example, Dental Colleges in Canada) have the legal responsibility for granting licenses but, in the end, these boards are usually controlled by dentists. For an arbitrary example, consider that the Arizona State Board of Dental Examiners comprises six dentists out of a total board of eleven. And the licensing boards are responsible not just for the licensing but also for the regulation, investigation and disciplining of dentists. In Canada the dental monopoly is further supported by recommended fee schedules put out by provincial dental associations. But each jurisdiction is different; for example, the American Dental Association is prohibited from recommending fees.

Society strictly enforces the dental monopoly by making it illegal for anyone to perform dental procedures without a dental license. In and of itself, such regulations are a good thing; they protect the consumer. But the system also concentrates power in few hands: complaints about a dentist's fitness or incompetence must be also dealt with by the licensing board. Yet there's nowhere to complain about absurdly high dental costs in jurisdictions where dental procedures are not covered by the state. It's a monopoly enshrined in law. J. D. Rockefeller would have been envious.

What about regulation? Do we as a society not regulate service levels or the fees dentists can charge just as monopolies like telephone and cable companies are regulated in many countries? No, we do not. For some reason we allow a dental monopoly to carry on virtually unchecked, depending on the Licensing Boards for self-regulation. We also allow dentists to have opaque pricing instead of insisting on posted fees. For example, there is no legal requirement for dentists to post a price list for common procedures. When I get a haircut, my barber lists the most commonly used services and fees at the front of his shop. Why doesn't my dentist? How else is a consumer to choose between dentists for the best value? How is a consumer to know if he is overcharged?

The only limit to what dentists charge is what individuals, companies and insurance providers are willing to tolerate in the extreme. With no real competition, the monopoly is a virtual license to print money at the expense of the rest of the population. And yet it is the electorate that should be able to control the monopoly. We're a democracy right? So why don't we?

Now let's take a step back to consider for a moment the other side of the argument. There will be those who will argue that, because of the many years of training required for dentists, it's reasonable to allow them to recoup their education costs and their income lost during training in the form of higher salaries. I agree completely. After all dentists are educated, well trained professionals. But remember that a dentist is not a businessman in the conventional sense. Because he's part of a protected monopoly, he has very little risk of failure; in fact he's virtually guaranteed success as long as he's competent. A businessman who makes a fortune is entitled to his gains because he's taken a big gamble on his business and has undertaken all its related risks. Success is not guaranteed; many businesses fail. Moreover, if a businessman is wildly successful other businesses will enter the market to compete with him. But because a dentist is part of a monopoly, he's not in the same category. Theoretically more students could enter dentistry and that could put downward pressure on pricing. But dentists train dentists so they have some control on the supply of new practitioners unless we force the issue through regulation. And there's also a long delay between accepting more dental students and seeing more dentists in the market. All this being said, because dentists are professionals we should not begrudge them a good living. But if they want to remain part of a protected monopoly, what they charge needs to be regulated lest it get out of hand.

None of this discussion is to suggest that there aren't good dentists who are in the profession in order to help people, although many of us know of dentists who are more concerned with their income than their patients. And none of this discussion is to suggest that there is a conspiracy of dentists attempting to take control of the country after they siphon off as much money as possible. But the problem is an insidious one. It's caused by a weak democratic system that does not consciously look out for the interests of society as a whole.

As a side note, very recently there has been some hope in Canada that the ratio of dentists to patients has been increasing and that dental prices will begin falling[22]. Perhaps I'm too cynical but I suspect this suggestion is the result of a rumor put out by the dental associations themselves. So whether true dental competition becomes a reality remains to be seen.

And the dentists are not alone. A single Bar Association is given a monopoly over representing clients in the legal system. It is also given a monopoly over the judiciary since only members of the Bar can become judges. With this cozy monopoly the legal profession, like others, seems to focus more on income and less on the value given to clients. Should not our government be regulating the legal profession just as it regulates any monopoly? Who hasn't heard the various jokes about a lawyer's billing methods?

A lawyer died and arrived at the [Pearly Gates][23]. To his dismay, there were thousands of people ahead of him in line to see St. Peter. But, to his surprise, St. Peter left his desk at the gate and came down the long line to where the lawyer was standing. St. Peter greeted him warmly. Then St. Peter and one of his assistants took the lawyer by the hands and guided him up to the front of the line into a comfortable chair by his desk.

---

[22] http://news.nationalpost.com/2013/03/25/glut-of-dentists-means-tough-times-for-them-good-deals-for-customers-doom-and-gloom-report-says

[23] http://www.ahajokes.com/law007.html

The lawyer said, "I don't mind all this attention, but what makes me so special?"

St. Peter replied, "Well, I've added up all the hours for which you billed your clients, and by my calculation you must be about 193 years old!"

Or who hasn't read a book where lawyers live a life of unabashed luxury? Think of John Grisham's "King of Torts," where lawyers compete to see who has the most extravagant possessions, including private jets. Lawyers take great pride in charging for their knowledge of our arcane legal system but many seem to take advantage of their monopoly by gouging their clients. And, as a profession, they certainly don't seem to make an effort to streamline the system.

Doctors have a similar monopoly to dentists. Engineers have a monopoly over public safety, although I must admit that engineers don't seem to take the same advantage of their clients as the other professions. I think that's because engineers differ from other professionals. I know many engineers. Perhaps they're different because they're just regular people with some mildly antisocial tendencies coupled with a touch of Attention Deficit Disorder (ADD). I'm not saying that all dentists, lawyers and doctors are bad. I'm just saying that, as a society, we have to be very careful about the monopolies we perpetuate. Remember Lord Acton's quotation about absolute power.

Many people would also argue that regulating doctors and dentists is unfair because, as health care workers, they are so altruistic. I believe this is a modern fiction rooted in a historical truth. A 1950s dentist was probably one who truly wanted to help people. I'm not implying that a 21st century dentist doesn't want to help people but because of the dental monopoly and the inflated income that comes with it, we implicitly encourage students to go into dentistry for the money, probably a bad reason for anyone to enter any health care profession. So another good side effect of proper regulation would be to discourage the get-rich-quick youth from choosing a serious profession when we need good souls rather than just ambitious or greedy souls. Personally, I'm more interested in a dentist that puts my health first and his bank account second.

So why does the world suck? Because our society doesn't have a proper system to keep monopolies in check when the natural behavior of a monopoly is to seize as many resources as it can for itself. The world sucks because we have bequeathed some groups the exclusive right to control an industry. And it sucks because our leaders are too weak or too well lobbied to protect society from these abuses.

12. UNFAIR JUSTICE

I think the first duty of society is justice.

—Alexander Hamilton 1755-1804
Founding Father of the United States

Why is our justice system unfair?

Star Trek depicts justice in the 24th century much as it is in the 21st, with independent judges and tribunals. Yet in Star Trek there doesn't seem to be any indication that the system is unfair. What about about our 21st century brand of justice?

Earlier we demonstrated the potential for injustice in a system where lawyers and judges are members of an exclusive monopolistic fraternity. There is no need to revisit that point but there are other reasons our justice system is unfair. Consider how the system doesn't properly respect the individual, the innocent individual in particular. In some jurisdictions an innocent man wrongly incarcerated for a major crime might eventually receive compensation, but what of an innocent victim of the system who is exonerated? What of the damages due to this victim? I'm not suggesting for an instant that a perfect justice system can be created but I am suggesting that the system should aim to do as little harm as possible. And if it does do harm, it should attempt to compensate for it.

Consider an example. You are arrested, detained and tried for a murder you didn't commit. You use all your available financial means to hire the best lawyer you can possibly afford. The lawyer does a first-rate job so, by the end of the long trial, you are acquitted. Has justice been served? The answer depends on what is really meant by the question. If I mean "Was the innocent person found innocent?" then the answer is "Yes, justice was served." But my question is actually more far reaching. It includes the concept that the justice system should do no harm to an innocent person. And to that question the answer must be a resounding "No, justice was not served."

True, you were exonerated. But the months you spent waiting for a verdict, whether in detention or at trial or at home on bail, caused you irreparable psychological trauma. After all, though you were innocent you knew full well that a guilty verdict was still a possibility. And what about the harm to your family, especially your children, and to your friends? And what about the financial burden of defending yourself against an accusation later proven to be false? And what of the damage to your career? You suffered harm because the justice system made a mistake. So how possibly can this be called justice?

Being a little more just

So how do we solve this problem? I believe the solution is obvious. The government (which after all brought the charges) should bear the financial cost of your defense. After all, this is what often happens in civil trials under the English Rule[24]. (Although the United States is one of the few countries that does not typically assign costs to the losing party, perhaps it too should consider it for criminal trials.) And assigning costs to the losing party would have a beneficial side effect on aggressive public prosecutors eager to climb the political ladder. If the prosecutor's office would shoulder the burden of a loss, would it not give a prosecutor pause before charging someone without sufficient evidence?

You might be thinking this approach will be very expensive.

---

[24] http://en.wikipedia.org/wiki/English_rule_(attorney's_fees)

How would the government pay for this added cost? One way would be for the court to levy a new fee on each case that would go into a special fund. Another way would be to make those found guilty to pay the prosecutor's costs, although many will not be able to do so. It might also be reasonable to let the judge decide whether the prosecutor's office should pay the defense's costs. And I'm sure there are other methods. The point here is that the government and the legal system should not be allowed to penalize individuals when it's the government itself which made a mistake. As in any market-driven system, there must be a penalty to the loser for being wrong. Nor should there be a financial penalty for being innocent. Perhaps, in addition to legal costs, the innocent should also be compensated for lost time and/or wages. Perhaps the innocent should also receive damages for suffering. All ideas would need to be evaluated by each individual jurisdiction.

I realize that there will be opponents to this approach and I can just imagine the arguments against protecting people financially from wrongful charges. The main arguments against it would no doubt be the cost to the public purse. But let us not forget one very important point here: the costs being incurred already exist. I'm not proposing that we add new systemic costs and then have the government pay for them. I'm only proposing that the side in the wrong shoulder the burden as occurs in civil trials under the English Rule. Until now we've simply passed these costs arbitrarily onto an innocent person because we can. How would you feel if it were you who was wrongfully charged? Or your spouse or parent or child? The ordeal would be bad enough without having to pay for defending yourself. These extra costs are burdensome to anyone unlucky enough to receive them. So why make a random citizen bear the costs? Should we not, as a society, insure ourselves against this sort of thing and agree that we must collectively share the burden rather than shoving it off on some unfortunate soul? And would the system not try harder to improve if it shoulders the costs?

Purchasing justice

The other problem with forcing an innocent person to shoulder the cost of his defense is that it's much harder on those of limited means. A rich man can easily afford the best defense but a poor man can't. The term "justice is blind" doesn't seem to apply to legal defense. In our society is justice blind only within an economic class? Since the poor receive court-appointed legal counsel, I suppose that's better than receiving no council at all. But the wealthy receive the best council, meaning the best lawyers, the best researchers, the best consultants and the best overall defense. For the poor, it means an overworked, underpaid lawyer who, even with the best of effort and intentions, has little if any support from researchers and consultants. It means the poor get at best a mediocre defense. Justice is clearly not blind regarding economic status.

So what do we do? It's a tough issue because taking away the right of the wealthy to defend themselves to the best of their financial ability does take something away from them. But the only way we have a chance of reforming an arrogant and unfair justice system is to treat the rich the same as we treat the poor. Why? Because the rich have the resources and the connections to force change in the system. So let's make everyone use the public defender. And let rich and poor alike push for change. Because the poor can't do it alone. And they're being shafted.

Other irritants

What else is unfair about our justice system? I think the arrogance of the system is unreasonable and disrespects our society. Few in the justice system seem concerned with the hardship the system itself places on individual citizens. And this disrespect endangers the goodwill of the citizenry. Another example seems appropriate.

A drunk driver

My wife and I were following what appeared to be a drunk driver one evening. The driver had great difficulty controlling the vehicle as we watched the car weave in and out of its lane. We called the police and provided the relevant information, including the license plate of the car we were following and our names and contact information.

Later that evening while we were at home the doorbell rang. A policeman stood outside the door and asked to speak with us. Once seated inside our home, he explained that the police had caught the driver, given him a Breathalyzer and had confirmed that he was legally drink. The policeman then asked if we would sign a complaint. When I asked what the ramifications of signing the complaint were to us he said that, since this driver had been charged with drunk driving six times before, the charge would most probably never get to court. We happily signed the complaint feeling we were doing our duty as citizens.

Some time passed but we each eventually received a subpoena to appear in court. Now, I'm not complaining about that one of us needed to go to court. I understand that the court needed to hear testimony first-hand. After all, civic duty was why we had called the police in the first place. But I am complaining about the two subpoenas which would cost us each a day's work. If the system were at all sympathetic to its citizens would it not have been reasonable to ask which of us was best able to attend the proceeding? Could not the witness who would be unable to attend provide an affidavit instead? Was the system not concerned that by abusing its privilege of sending us each a subpoena that we would become bitter and no longer be interested in doing our bit in the future?

This may all seem awfully minor but it really isn't. And what happened later made a further mockery of the system itself. On the court date we drove downtown, parked the car and found the courtroom. When we entered the court we made ourselves known to the prosecutor and took our seats. It's this next bit which really rattles me. When the judge appeared in the courtroom he decided that he didn't like his chair. So while we all (prosecutors, lawyers, witnesses) waited, the court clerk went to the adjacent courtroom to find the judge a new chair. In fact, the clerk tried several chairs and each time the judge left the courtroom and reentered everyone in the courtroom had to stand up. Finally, after about fifteen minutes and several instances of "please rise" and "be seated," the judge was satisfied and we could finally begin. Yet after all these shenanigans, our trial never even took place. When the accused learned that there was a witness in the courtroom he pleaded guilty and cut a deal with the prosecutor. So what about us? We had both lost a valuable day. We were simply told unceremoniously to leave. Other than the original arresting police officer, no one ever thanked us for coming or in any way acknowledged the time we had lost to the exercise.

Furthermore, society now had at least one person (me) who would be reluctant to get involved again. I'm not saying I wouldn't get involved in the future but I am saying that I would be reticent and I would have to consider the situation carefully. Before this nonsense, I would not have hesitated. Because of the arrogance of the system, society may have lost an ally.

The perp walk

Returning to the plight of an innocent victim of the justice system, some jurisdictions make no effort to protect the privacy of someone accused of a crime. I don't see a need to protect the identity of someone who has been convicted but an accused person is innocent until proven guilty and his privacy must surely be respected.

A very good example of this issue and the difference between jurisdictions was the 2011 Strauss-Kahn case in New York. Dominique Strauss-Kahn, a French citizen, was arrested on charges of sexual assault and attempted rape. The charges never went to trial but the police allowed the media to photograph Strauss-Kahn when he was arrested during what is known as a "perp walk." Such an invasion of privacy is illegal in France and was thoroughly condemned in the French media. At the time of his arrest Strauss-Kahn was a potential Presidential candidate in France so the American lack of respect for his privacy probably destroyed his candidacy. Whether M. Strauss-Kahn was guilty or innocent is not at issue. His case never went to trial. But the behavior of the American authorities, in a country that rightly prides itself on individual rights, is nothing less than shameful.

Children's Aid

For one final irritant, let's highlight a topic that I touched on in one of the first few chapters: Children's Aid, also called Child Protective Services. In many civilized countries Children's Aid Societies have been empowered to protect children from abuse, a laudable goal in and of itself. Unfortunately, in some countries these organizations have been given powers so broad that Joseph Stalin might have been envious had he known about them. Since laws vary from one jurisdiction to another, let's consider one the most egregious abuses of this power in the Western world. And it occurs in what would seem to be a very civilized jurisdiction: Ontario, Canada.

In Ontario, Children's Aid Societies have virtually unlimited power; their caseworkers have "as much power as God[25]." They can enter a home without a warrant, apprehend a child without due process, insist police enforce apprehensions even when the police don't agree, order medication of a child and deny parental access. Despite all this power to protect children, Children's Aid has left children with foster parents known to be dangerous. Not surprisingly perhaps, since Children's Aid is funded on a per child

---

[25]   http://fullcomment.nationalpost.com/2013/02/27/barbara-kay-the-problem-with-childrens-aid-societies

basis, these organizations have an incentive to take children into custody. More information can be found on the disgraceful state of Children's Aid in Ontario from an award-winning documentary entitled "Powerful as God[26]" available at the blakout.ca website. Though Ontario might be the worst example, it's not alone with these problems. These organizations have sweeping powers across Canada. In the United States the equivalent organizations are called Child Protective Services and they also have problems.

We're so proud of our advanced legal system that protects the innocent but whatever happened to "innocent until proven guilty"? Why can Children's Aid remove a child from his home without any evidence and without any court involvement? We wouldn't allow a policeman to search our house without probable cause or a warrant so why would we allow a caseworker to seize our children? This may not be allowed in your jurisdiction but consider this point: neither Canada nor the United States is a backward country yet the system can allow this kind of unreasonable and hypocritical behavior. Even though most people would probably agree that this is unfair and that it shouldn't happen, they probably don't know about it. So the system does what it wants even if it tramples on the rights of its citizens. Isn't it time to make our systems more responsible to and respectful of the people?

So why does the world suck? Because even our justice system, a system designed to keep us safe, can do more harm than good. It sucks because it doesn't even follow its own rules. It sucks because there are straightforward ways to avoid the worst of its ill effects yet we, as citizens, have done little to improve the system.

---

[26]   http://blakout.ca/htm/viewthedoc.php#.Ufa-hl3VB8E

13. MORTALITY, EDUCATION & OPPORTUNITY

In this world nothing can be said to be certain, except death and taxes.

−Benjamin Franklin 1706-1790
Founding Father of the United States

Why think about mortality?

Our mortality defines us today and will continue to define us in the future. Star Trek tried to explore immortality on several occasions but that was fiction; in the real world, mortality is something that is simply not going to change. Certainly not for the foreseeable future.

Since I was a young child I have always looked to the end of my life. I believe this outlook started when I watched a program about the future when I was about seven years old. The program attempted to predict what our world would be like in the year 2000. It proved remarkably prescient, predicting home computers, flat screen monitors, personal phones and Bricklin-style automobiles. Since watching that program I waited anxiously for the various predictions to come true while I also counted down the years remaining until the year 2000. After the year 2000 I began to estimate the percentage of my life remaining.

You might think such an estimate is morbid but it's not; I often calculate the time remaining until various events and I often calculate using percentages rather than raw values. I'm not trying to excuse this behavior; perhaps I just do it because I'm nuts ... after all, even my wife says I'm crazy! The point here is that, like most people, I know my life is finite and that simple realization defines the way I look at the world.

The way we look at the world is important. Religious and nonreligious people might look at death differently but both know that their lives are finite. They might well therefore come to the same conclusion: that the meaning of our lives must be defined by more than just the simple acts we perform while we are alive. A life of unabashed luxury might be enjoyable but it drains resources from our world and the enjoyment dies with its host. A life of crime or of condescension or of abuse contributes to the world only when it is extinguished. But a life of honesty or of charity or of kindness leaves behind it something eternal. If during our lives we work diligently and do the best we can, then we contribute to the world. If we raise our children well, then they and their children will continue to contribute to the world. If we honor our promises and encourage others to do the same, then we also contribute to a better world.

I am not suggesting that we try to be saints; a life of complete sacrifice is for most not a life worth living. But if it comes down to a choice between enjoyment or honor, then to give our lives purpose we must surely choose honor. Animals don't understand honor so we can rise above our animal behavior by being honorable. History is full of nasty people who enjoyed their lives but made the lives of others miserable. Certainly Joseph Stalin, Ferdinand Marcos, and Kim Jong-il all lived well enough. Ask yourself: would you enslave or kill others to maximize your own enjoyment?

To my detractors the suggestion to choose honor over enjoyment might seem socialist, but it isn't. I'm not suggesting that this choice be mandated by society. Nor is it a form of religion because I'm not implying the force of a higher power. This is a personal choice that I believe society should simply encourage. Some people will take that choice; some won't. But I suspect that those who live by a code of honor will have fewer regrets on their deathbeds.

Some people believe life is just a competition to see who can accumulate the most. I believe they are partially correct. Life is indeed a competition but it's not a competition with others; it's a competition with ourselves. It's a competition to see how well we can each rise above our animal pedigree, to improve the world and to leave the world better than we found it. Again, this isn't socialism; some of the best-known charitable people are also the most capitalist (e.g. Rockefeller, Gates, Buffet). Being a good, honorable person is simply the ultimate state we can achieve.

So why think about mortality? Because if we were immortal then our outlook would change. We would then have infinite time to achieve all our goals. But realizing that we are mortal and that our lives are short, we know that what we can do during are lives is very limited. We should therefore try to leave behind something good of ourselves that endures forever, something which will help ensure that our society has the best possible chance to prosper.

Basic Education

Recognizing our mortality also helps us realize how important education is to society. The knowledge and skills we accumulate during our lives die with us unless we somehow pass them along. That's the purpose of education. As a society we must therefore be very careful how we manage the education process in order to optimize the transfer of knowledge to the next generation.

Western civilization currently gives all its members a basic education. Children learn to read and write. They learn other languages. They learn history and geography. They learn mathematics. And they learn about science. Education is mandatory and free until children are about 18 years old. We do this to ensure an educated, productive society. We do this to ensure that basic knowledge is passed through the generations. So far so good.

Unfortunately the quality of basic education is not always consistent. Wealthy children may attend private schools which often provide a superior education. But even children attending public schools experience a wide range of standards and it is the wealthier neighborhoods that usually have the better schools. This is not only unfair to those children attending inferior schools, it is bad for our society. If poor families have uneducated children then chances are those children will remain poor. We then risk social instability by creating a perpetual underclass. And we risk losing our best and brightest if we do not provide everyone with the best education we can.

Consider a hypothetical situation. Imagine that in 25 years' time a large meteor will approach Earth. At that time scientists unanimously agree that, when it hits, it will destroy the planet and all life on it. The meteor is so large and moving so fast that scientists and engineers do not have a way to avoid the collision. Oops. Now return to today and imagine that a very, very bright student is attending a mediocre inner city school. The student loves mathematics and science but he is bored with the curriculum and his teachers are too busy to keep him interested. As a result, at age 16 he decides to quit school to work in a computer store. If we were omnipotent we might see that, if this same student had been given a more enlightened education, he might have eventually received a doctorate in engineering and eventually worked on space exploration. In 25 years' time that same student might have been able to stop the destruction of Earth. Had he been given a proper education.

Genius knows no economic bounds but we need to nurture it for it to blossom. If we don't, then we don't give our society the best chance for growth. And our lack of foresight may even cause our own demise.

Let's briefly revisit a comment I made in an earlier chapter about the children of welfare recipients having the opportunity to avoid welfare themselves. If we guarantee a decent education for all children, then there's no need for any child born into welfare to remain dependent on the state. But if we don't actively manage the quality of education, history shows us that poor children will be the ones who suffer and that we will be perpetuating an underclass. Again, this is not socialism. It's pragmatism. Though true success must come from ability and hard work, we can't afford to discard some of our best young resources just because they're poor.

Higher Education

It's true that basic education is a problem but it's on higher education that we really fall down. Post-secondary education is rarely free nowadays though, as you will see, that's not necessarily a bad thing. We need to ensure that our best and brightest receive a decent university education, something that can be ensured through scholarships and bursaries. Those on the socialist side of the political spectrum might prefer a free high education for everyone but we know that this approach wastes resources and results in poor standards. Education is no different than any other area of the economy ... it improves with competition. Those on the capitalist side of the political spectrum might prefer that everyone pay the same fees but we know that the best and brightest cannot always afford higher education.

The wealthy can afford to send their children to the best universities even if the experience is wasted. But even the wealthy, were they to take a step back, must admit that using money to put a child through a wasted education is a horrible misuse of resources. It's a waste for the child, a waste for the parent, a waste for the university and a waste for society. Money can buy luxuries but money should not be able to misallocate society's most important resources.

So what to do? I suggest letting all colleges and universities be run independent of the state so they can compete independently for students and fees. But education is too important to society to let the wealthy gobble up all the best educational resources. Let the government therefore manage these resources in a way that is fair to everyone yet still satisfies the wealthiest families' desire to send even a substandard monster to a good university.

Managing Opportunity

The answer to managing higher education lies with a means to subsidize the best students so society does not lose these precious minds. Years ago in many countries students paid a small portion of the actual cost of their education or nothing at all. The problem with this approach was that the subsidy was available to all students, no matter how good they were or how much they would benefit from the curriculum. More recently tuition has been raised dramatically to reflect a larger percentage of the actual cost of providing the education, though a portion of the extra funds have been used to expand scholarships and bursaries. With the additional scholarships and bursaries, subsidies have shifted toward the brightest and neediest students. This emphasis is surely a better way to allocate resources than providing assistance to those who wouldn't benefit. Unfortunately, we haven't gone far enough.

Higher education isn't like basic education. Everyone needs a basic education to function in and contribute to society. But higher education is for the academically inclined: a waste for those who are not and a boon for those who are. To my mind the way to deal with higher education funding is as follows. Let universities charge market rates that reflect not only their excellence but also the demand for their services. But because education is a key societal resource, each university should be required to provide a number of scholarships and bursaries based on student need and ability. Universities have always offered scholarships of their own accord to attract the best students, but bursaries don't boost ratings. Both subsidies need to be enshrined in law. The bursary guidelines can be drawn up by each jurisdiction but it's important that they should be based on a combination of need and ability. The goal is to make sure society encourages its best and brightest to contribute to their full potential.

Consider Mary who was raised by her single mother and who is in the top 2% of students academically. She wants to be a pediatrician but she has no savings of her own and her mother can barely afford to pay half the total tuition required for a medical degree. It would be a shame if society did not afford Mary the opportunity to become a pediatrician. Both Mary and society would lose were that to happen. Even if loans were available, it would be society's loss if Mary did not pursue her medical career. So, although she has some financial resources, because of her outstanding academic credentials a student like Mary should be awarded a scholarship. We need to encourage Mary to become a pediatrician.

Scott is not a good student, being in the bottom 25% of students academically. He was raised in an orphanage and has no savings nor a sponsor to help with tuition. He wants to be a physiotherapist although it may be difficult for him to find a college that will accept him. It's simply not in society's interest to support Scott's goal financially since the funds could be better spent on stronger students. Although Scott is in a poorer financial position than Mary, it's unlikely that a public investment in Scott would pay off and might displace a more promising candidate. That doesn't mean that Scott should not be afforded other opportunities or other types of support, just that some sort of grant for Scott's college tuition is not the best use of available funds.

Allison is a horrible student, being in the bottom 10% of students academically. But her parents are very wealthy, her mother part of the third generation of an energy and chemicals dynasty. Of course there's no hope of Allison receiving either a scholarship or a bursary. The question is whether society should allow Allison's parents to pay for her education and thereby take valuable resources away from others. I believe this should be allowed but that the market should deal with it. The college or university that accepts Allison will have to make a calculation as to what tuition Allison will have to pay to be accepted. Perhaps she will have to pay double the standard tuition or perhaps her parents will have to set up a special trust for less fortunate students. Regardless, the university itself will decide based on what is good for the institution and whatever decision the university makes will mean that Allison's parents will contribute more resources to the university than it would lose by accepting her. Better to allow each university to make its own decisions and let competition keep the system honest, than to let a government bureaucrat make the decision. Or be bribed to do so.

Again, this discussion about education is not about socialism versus capitalism. Society can choose either approach regarding the management of companies or natural resources or medical care. But education is different because education is our future. If we had unlimited resources, then money would not be a problem and each child would be able to choose his own path. But because resources are limited, society needs to direct them where they are most likely to yield positive results. In the same way, society should also encourage and support those who excel in nonacademic areas to pursue their goals. But whatever we do we must stop needlessly squandering the resources that will define our future.

Other opportunities

Unfortunately education isn't the only area in which society is inefficient at managing resources. A degree from a prestigious university can dramatically increase someone's chances of getting a good job at a good company. This happens everywhere in the world because of what is called the "Old Boy Network." In the United States we've heard of this happening with graduates from well-known universities such as Harvard and Yale. In England similar advantages are available from Cambridge and Oxford. It's a shame. Although these universities may indeed provide an excellent education, the real differentiator for any job applicant is surely the applicant himself. Being in the Old Boy Network is like being royalty or being the heir to a large fortune. When the advantages of blood or connections outweigh merit, our society begins a slippery slope of decline. The only good news here is that companies that support such inefficient hiring practices put themselves at a disadvantage relative to their competitors. At least that's a little good news from the market system.

So why does the world suck? It sucks because we continue to misallocate one of our most precious resource: education. And we allow money and connections to override merit.

Why the World Sucks

14. MAKING IT A REALITY

You must be the change you wish to see in the world.

– Mahatma Gandhi 1869-1948
Indian independence movement leader

Experimenting with democracy

Star Trek provides many examples of how to experiment with new systems of government. It provides examples of colonies that eschew technology, colonies that use genetic engineering and colonies that are designed from the ground up. Moving a group of people to an uninhabited planet to create a new civilization might be an attractive solution in the 24th century, but it's simply not possible today with our existing technology. So to change our system we need to devise a different solution.

Making what a reality?

Throughout this book I've identified several systemic problems with Western democracies. Our laws are so numerous, so complex, so inconsistent and so hypocritical that many of us have lost respect for them. Our electoral system unfairly gives some voters the right to improve their lot at the expense of the rest of the population. Our leaders are encouraged to lie with impunity. Our governments gridlock themselves to the detriment of the people they serve. We give certain groups the right to abuse their monopoly positions enshrined in law. Our justice system is arrogant and disrespectful, forces costs on the innocent and shirks a duty to protect privacy. Our best and brightest children are not given the opportunities that they deserve. Nice, isn't it?

And what about the non-systemic problems I have listed in this book? What about the lack of honesty in our society? Or lack of honor? Do we not need to address these issues as well? We do but I don't believe there is a direct means to improve the way individuals look at themselves and their world. We can't legislate honorable behavior directly. Yet our views are surely shaped by the way the system deals with transgressions of such ideals. For example, it's difficult to explain to a child why lying is wrong when he sees for himself that his leaders lie. So my hope (and perhaps even my expectation) is that, if we improve the system, individual views and behavior will also improve.

So what reality are we aiming for? As I've said all along, I cannot provide a perfect answer since this book is more about questions and ideas. But looking back over earlier chapters, I can make a few suggestions that may go a long way to improving our chances for the future. Remember that these are suggestions, not solutions:

1. *Voters must pass a Citizenship test.* How many times have you found that naturalized citizens understand how the system works better than those born here? That's because in most countries new citizens must pass a citizenship test. But the system must require a minimum level of understanding of all its voters, otherwise voting is meaningless. Each voter must understand that with privilege comes responsibility, that voting is an honorable duty not a party joke. Making a citizenship course an integral part of a secondary school education would be immensely helpful. But for those who did not receive the course in school, the test must not be disadvantageous to the poor or uneducated. Citizenship education must therefore be free and widely available.

2. *A constitutional requirement that laws be minimalist and*

consistent. An independent tribunal or a legislative committee could be responsible for regularly reviewing laws and recommending which laws should be simplified or expunged.

3. *A set of public accountability requirements.* These would include various ideas proposed earlier including a candidate manifesto, better supervision and enforcement of public officials, and much harsher penalties for those who abuse the public trust.

4. *Jurisdiction changes.* A democratic world government to handle planet-wide concerns would be nice but much smaller jurisdictions would create a more competitive environment for public services.

5. *Stringent anti-monopoly regulation and enforcement.* Include quasopolies and licensed professions in the list of monopolies to be regulated.

6. *True justice.* Ensure judicial respect for citizens, strict privacy rules until conviction and compensation for the innocent.

7. *Targeted education reform.* Basic education with common standards for all. Full cost tuition for higher education with significant scholarships and bursaries to encourage the brightest and the needy.

Can change happen from within?

You may not agree with all of the above suggestions but you probably agree that we have serious problems that need to be fixed. So how do we push for improvement? Since we live in a democracy, one obvious possibility is to use the democratic process. It's a wonderfully straightforward idea but my suspicion is that it probably won't work. The electorate has shown time and time again that it's incapable of supporting change until there is absolutely no choice. It seems we would have to hit a brick wall first. Recall Greece?

That doesn't mean we shouldn't try. Teaching citizenship to our children and educating the electorate is a good starting point and can help. But it takes time. Supporting politicians with a track record of blunt honesty rather than those who just promise what we want to hear would also help. But the fact is that making significant changes in a democracy is incredibly difficult. And very, very slow.

Forcing change from outside

What else to do? Not revolution? No, something much more civilized.

You might consider the following suggestion somewhat eccentric. The alternative to democratic change from within is to again turn to the market system. What if we were to create from scratch a better independent democracy elsewhere and let competition force change in the other existing democracies? You might now be thinking about my disclaimer from the Preface where I said I was nuts. And that may cause you to have an issue with this idea because it's a wee bit unconventional. But I maintain it's a good idea. No, I think it's a great idea. And I think it can work under the right circumstances.

Neulandt

I suggest creating a new country. For now let's all it "Neulandt." This country would be set up from its inception to have small jurisdictions that can operate relatively independently. All the ideas I have listed in this book can be easily enshrined in a constitution including the educational, electoral, and judicial processes we have discussed. But how to start a country from scratch? I see two possibilities.

The first possibility has been proposed by others before,[27] and

---

[27] http://www.thesun.co.uk/sol/homepage/news/3774868/Billionaire-to-build-new-

that is to construct a new country on a floating platform in international waters. My problem with this idea is that I'm not certain how many people would want to live there. I don't know if you would relish the idea of living on a platform floating in the ocean. I know I wouldn't.

The second possibility is to purchase land from an existing country to create an independent state. I like this idea better for several reasons. First, I believe Neulandt's founding citizens would like to live on solid ground. Second, any country willing to sell some of its land to a new sovereign state is probably quite poor. By buying the land instead of building a platform, Neulandt would be helping a poor country financially, something that's a worthwhile endeavor on its own.

So far so good. But where will the money come from? I believe the key to financing this project lies in the fact that the creation of a new country is an unusual event these days. All the land on our little blue planet has been claimed by one jurisdiction or another, sometimes by more than one. Although new countries are occasionally created, they are usually not really new countries but rather the result of a division; e.g. South Sudan. So I believe that many people would be very interested in being a founding father (or mother) to a new country. Imagine if you could be considered a George Washington or Benjamin Franklin for all eternity. It's a rare opportunity for immortality. Look at all those millionaires and billionaires willing to shell out for a trip into orbit or to the Moon or to Mars. The creation of a new country might well be a crazy concept but it provides a unique opportunity to be part of history.

You now know where the money is to come from. The wealthiest people on the planet, those with hundreds of millions or billions of disposable Dollars or Euros or Reminbi or Shekels are no doubt aching to be founding fathers to a new country. To make

---

countries-at-sea.html

this idea a little more concrete, I propose that a founding father, say someone who contributes at least 250 million dollars, should have his name written in the constitution and be accorded automatic citizenship in Neulandt. Furthermore, only a portion of the contribution need be a donation. The rest could be an investment in the country, like a bond, that would be repaid over a period of time with a specified rate of interest. Since the money contributed would not in its entirety be a gift, this would greatly increase the amount that could be raised.

And the new country would need a lot of money. Neulandt would not only have to purchase its land and compensate any persons displaced, but funds would be needed to develop a complete infrastructure from scratch before populating it with the best citizens to be found elsewhere. "Best" citizens is a vague description to be sure but, like any country, Neulandt will have to decide its own immigration criteria.

You might well ask about the indigenous population that Neulandt will displace. To be fair beyond reproach, I propose that each person living in the area to be taken over by Neulandt be given a choice: relocate elsewhere in the original country with a handsome payment or be offered citizenship in the new country. Either way, the entire indigenous population would benefit from the transaction and no one would be forced to leave.

Setting up Neulandt

Before properly becoming an operating country, Neulandt would have to create a provisional government to write a constitution, purchase its land and begin the design and construction of an infrastructure. This government would also have to begin soliciting immigration applications from potential citizens in countries around the world. Remember that this new country would want to recruit the best of every discipline. Of course it would recruit the best doctors, nurses, lawyers, teachers, judges, engineers. But it would also recruit the best policemen, carpenters, electricians, maids and janitors. The attraction of Neulandt would be its dedication to efficiency and its design for political choice. Each county would initially have its own political philosophy so no one would be stuck with the mediocre politics of an overall majority. After that, politics would evolve as in any market driven system. Even if you don't support the idea, you might well agree that it would be an interesting experiment.

The effect of Neulandt

Initially Neulandt might well be the butt of dinnertime jokes. But I suspect that it would eventually have a profound effect on other democracies. What follows is only supposition to be sure, but sooner or later I believe other countries would find to their dismay that some of their best and brightest had moved to Neulandt. And then it would be a joke no longer. As more of the best minds and bodies left their home countries it would become a point of serious discussion and the other democracies would have to discuss change. They would have to address their deficiencies. Or so I think. Or so I hope.

Neulandt is just an idea. There's no real plan and there's no real sponsorship. But imagine if it could be done. And imagine the effect on the rest of the world.

Why the World Sucks

15. WRAP UP

The difficulty lies not so much in developing new ideas
as in escaping from old ones.

—John Maynard Keynes 1883-1946
  British economist

Congratulations

If you have gotten this far then congratulations. I warned you from the beginning that this book would be a little different. I warned you that I'm nuts and that this book might be a bit dry in places and a little preachy in others. But I hope you found some of my observations informative and some of my recommendations interesting. Our world is what we make of it and too many people simply accept it the way it is. That's a shameful attitude because we're not making use of our potential as human beings if we don't try to improve ourselves and the system we live in.

I've made no bones about it: I detest the world we live in today. I find it not only inefficient but irrational, unfair and unreasonable. Our leaders are liars. Those in privileged positions try to grab ever more for themselves. Those in collective bargaining units depict "merit" as a dirty word and try to coerce those who would rather be independent. The nastiest people reap the rewards of their deceptions. The best people are short-changed. The system harms the innocent without trying to make things right. But worst of all, some of our best and brightest are so disillusioned that they do not contribute properly or at all.

Conservatives come across as selfish. Liberals come across as lazy. Surely there's a way to use common sense to do the right thing. I hope some of my suggestions point a light in that direction.

My suggestion for Neulandt isn't meant to be fiction. I truly do think it's a constructive way to influence the world even if it is a formidable task. But, like so many of my ideas, I think Neulandt, though a good idea, is still only half-baked. Well, perhaps quarter-baked. It will be a gargantuan task to create a new country, but I believe it's a noble one.

I think we can improve our world if each of us tries to change it just a little bit. If you agree and have found value in this book then I ask that you spread the ideas to your friends, acquaintances, colleagues and family. And I encourage you to add your own ideas to the mix. By all means recommend this book as well if you wish, but it's the ideas that are important. Let's stop accepting canned political ideas from the left or from the right and let's just start solving the problems in front of us. Then we won't have to look to Star Trek for solutions; we'll have made our own.

ABOUT THE AUTHOR

Find out more about B Regan Asher on the author's website at http://breganasher.com. On the website you will also find out more about novels like "Il Vendetta" and "White Cell." And about the short story "Why I Had to Kill My Brother."

Il Vendetta

When a buyer was murdered in rural Pennsylvania, the secret world of Star Stores began to unravel. With almost a trillion dollars in sales, the company had completely concealed its clandestine operations. But now suppliers in China were starting to fight back. And, in the US, one lone man would choose to speak out. It was then a race against time to go public before the retailer could stop him.

White Cell

Hackers are a little strange and Jim Kincaid is no different. Deep in debt, he loans money from the uncle of an acquaintance. Now he's drawn into a world of Mafia and terrorism, a world which threatens his family and friends. Somehow he must free himself from this situation and, in so doing, learn the secret from his past which will explain so much.

Why I Had to Kill My Brother

I grew up in a good family with my brother Emory and two sisters. Our parents had taught us well, not only the difference between right and wrong, but also the importance of looking after family. Family was very important; family was everything. So when I decided to join Emory in a business venture I wasn't worried. I trusted my brother.

But I shouldn't have.

For the way I was treated, I needed retribution. I sought revenge for the way he crippled me emotionally and for the strain he put on my other family relationships. He affected my health and he destroyed my outlook on life. I needed to show him what he had done. I had to punish him.

To get my life back, I had to take his.

About B Regan Asher

The author behind B Regan Asher has worked in many different fields, from space engineering to commercial manufacturing to financial algorithms to software development. He has incorporated his personal experience into each of the books he has written.

The author lives with his wife and two children in Ontario, Canada and welcomes comments and inquiries through his website's contact form at http://breganasher.com/contact.